CalmUp®
JOURNEY
PAGES

CALMUP® Journey

Also by Lorie S. Gose, Psy.D.

CalmUp® Journey: Your Daily Ascending Tool for Better Days
Published by Balboa Press

CalmUp®
JOURNEY PAGES

Your Keepsafe for Better Days

Lorie S. Gose, Psy.D.

BALBOA
PRESS

A DIVISION OF HAY HOUSE

Balboa Press books may be ordered through booksellers or by contacting:

Balboa Press
A Division of Hay House
1663 Liberty Drive
Bloomington, IN 47403
www.balboapress.com
1 (877) 407-4847

Because of the dynamic nature of the Internet, any web addresses or links contained in this book may have changed since publication and may no longer be valid. The views expressed in this work are solely those of the author and do not necessarily reflect the views of the publisher, and the publisher hereby disclaims any responsibility for them.

The author of this book does not dispense medical advice or prescribe the use of any technique as a form of treatment for physical, emotional, or medical problems without the advice of a physician, either directly or indirectly. The intent of the author is only to offer information of a general nature to help you in your quest for emotional and spiritual well-being. In the event you use any of the information in this book for yourself, which is your constitutional right, the author and the publisher assume no responsibility for your actions.

Copy Editing: Marj Hahne
Logo Design: Debbie Oberhausen
Cover Design: Andrew Mays
Book Design: Katie Schneider
Author Photograph: Stephanie Block

Certain stock imagery © Thinkstock.
Any people depicted in stock imagery provided by Thinkstock are models,
and such images are being used for illustrative purposes only.

ISBN: 978-1-4525-3450-3 (e)
ISBN: 978-1-4525-3449-7 (sc)

Library of Congress Control Number: 2011906326

Printed in the United States of America

Balboa Press rev. date: 8/17/2011

About CalmUp® Journey Pages

CalmUp® Journey Pages: Your Keepsafe for Better Days is the companion book to *CalmUp® Journey: Your Daily Ascending Tool for Better Days*. The foundational manual contains instructions and samples for completing the CalmUp® Journey. Further support, information, and resources are available at www.drloriegose.com.

CalmUp® Journey Pages holds a season's worth of your own CalmUp® Journeys, with consideration of the suggestion that you take one day off per week.

May these pages be your blank slate on which you create your better days. And may today always be your best day.

CalmUp® Journey

Date: _____

Instructions: Begin in the bottom row. Enter your responses, moving up from left to right.

Deep healing breath; conscious choices **FINISH** → *(1) Today I choose to empower myself by* *(2) I share/serve by*	‾‾‾‾‾‾‾ Peace & joy rating 1–10 (low to high)
Spirit	**Spirit**
Illusions (First clear your mind on the back of this page.) *I believed*	Creative openings *I open to*
Society	**Society**
Poor choices impacting others *My poor choices have included*	Being of service *With integrity, I will*
Inward	**Inward**
Disheartening image *I have pictured myself*	Self-loving visualization *Today I visualize myself*
Live	**Live**
Disturbing physical symptoms *I have experienced*	Positive affirmation for your health *I am*
Birth	**Birth**
Painful emotions *I have felt*	Peaceful emotions *As my authentic self, I feel*
One issue **START** → *How can I*	‾‾‾‾‾‾‾ Peace & joy rating 1–10 (low to high)

*Can you conceive that your responses in the left column are not "bad" and those in the right column are not "good"? We need **all** parts of ourselves to create our wholeness.*

Clear your mind by listing or journaling all your <u>worries, fears, and discouraging thoughts</u> about your question.

Allow your mind to become radiant by <u>brainstorming encouraging and hopeful ideas</u> about your question. What statements might a best friend, lover, or counselor offer?

CalmUp® Journey

Date: _____

Instructions: Begin in the bottom row. Enter your responses, moving up from left to right.

<u>Deep healing breath; conscious choices</u> **FINISH →** *(1) Today I choose to empower myself by* *(2) I share/serve by*	 ‾‾‾‾‾‾ Peace & joy rating 1–10 (low to high)
## Spirit	## Spirit
<u>Illusions</u> (First clear your mind on the back of this page.) *I believed*	<u>Creative openings</u> *I open to*
## Society	## Society
<u>Poor choices impacting others</u> *My poor choices have included*	<u>Being of service</u> *With integrity, I will*
## Inward	## Inward
<u>Disheartening image</u> *I have pictured myself*	<u>Self-loving visualization</u> *Today I visualize myself*
## Live	## Live
<u>Disturbing physical symptoms</u> *I have experienced*	<u>Positive affirmation for your health</u> *I am*
## Birth	## Birth
<u>Painful emotions</u> *I have felt*	<u>Peaceful emotions</u> *As my authentic self, I feel*
<u>One issue</u> **START →** *How can I*	 ‾‾‾‾‾‾ Peace & joy rating 1–10 (low to high)

Can you conceive that your responses in the left column are not "bad" and those in the right column are not "good"? We need <u>all</u> parts of ourselves to create our wholeness.

Clear your mind by listing or journaling all your <u>worries, fears, and discouraging thoughts</u> about your question.

Allow your mind to become radiant by <u>brainstorming encouraging and hopeful ideas</u> about your question. What statements might a best friend, lover, or counselor offer?

CalmUp® Journey

Date: _____

Instructions: Begin in the bottom row. Enter your responses, moving up from left to right.

Deep healing breath; conscious choices **FINISH →** *(1) Today I choose to empower myself by* *(2) I share/serve by*	 _____ Peace & joy rating 1–10 (low to high)
Spirit	**Spirit**
Illusions (First clear your mind on the back of this page.) *I believed*	Creative openings *I open to*
Society	**Society**
Poor choices impacting others *My poor choices have included*	Being of service *With integrity, I will*
Inward	**Inward**
Disheartening image *I have pictured myself*	Self-loving visualization *Today I visualize myself*
Live	**Live**
Disturbing physical symptoms *I have experienced*	Positive affirmation for your health *I am*
Birth	**Birth**
Painful emotions *I have felt*	Peaceful emotions *As my authentic self, I feel*
One issue **START →** *How can I*	 _____ Peace & joy rating 1–10 (low to high)

Can you conceive that your responses in the left column are not "bad" and those in the right column are not "good"? We need <u>all</u> parts of ourselves to create our wholeness.

Clear your mind by listing or journaling all your <u>worries, fears, and discouraging thoughts</u> about your question.

Allow your mind to become radiant by <u>brainstorming encouraging and hopeful ideas</u> about your question. What statements might a best friend, lover, or counselor offer?

CalmUp® Journey

Date: _____

Instructions: Begin in the bottom row. Enter your responses, moving up from left to right.

<u>Deep healing breath; conscious choices</u> **FINISH** → *(1) Today I choose to empower myself by* *(2) I share/serve by*	 _____ Peace & joy rating 1–10 (low to high)
Spirit	**Spirit**
<u>Illusions</u> (First clear your mind on the back of this page.) *I believed*	<u>Creative openings</u> *I open to*
Society	**Society**
<u>Poor choices impacting others</u> *My poor choices have included*	<u>Being of service</u> *With integrity, I will*
Inward	**Inward**
<u>Disheartening image</u> *I have pictured myself*	<u>Self-loving visualization</u> *Today I visualize myself*
Live	**Live**
<u>Disturbing physical symptoms</u> *I have experienced*	<u>Positive affirmation for your health</u> *I am*
Birth	**Birth**
<u>Painful emotions</u> *I have felt*	<u>Peaceful emotions</u> *As my authentic self, I feel*
 <u>One issue</u> **START** → *How can I*	 _____ Peace & joy rating 1–10 (low to high)

Can you conceive that your responses in the left column are not "bad" and those in the right column are not "good"? We need all parts of ourselves to create our wholeness.

Clear your mind by listing or journaling all your <u>worries, fears, and discouraging thoughts</u> about your question.

Allow your mind to become radiant by <u>brainstorming encouraging and hopeful ideas</u> about your question. What statements might a best friend, lover, or counselor offer?

CalmUp® Journey

Date: _____

Instructions: Begin in the bottom row. Enter your responses, moving up from left to right.

Deep healing breath; conscious choices **FINISH** → *(1) Today I choose to empower myself by* *(2) I share/serve by*	 ‾‾‾‾‾‾‾‾ Peace & joy rating 1–10 (low to high)
Spirit	**Spirit**
<u>Illusions</u> (First clear your mind on the back of this page.) *I believed*	<u>Creative openings</u> *I open to*
Society	**Society**
<u>Poor choices impacting others</u> *My poor choices have included*	<u>Being of service</u> *With integrity, I will*
Inward	**Inward**
<u>Disheartening image</u> *I have pictured myself*	<u>Self-loving visualization</u> *Today I visualize myself*
Live	**Live**
<u>Disturbing physical symptoms</u> *I have experienced*	<u>Positive affirmation for your health</u> *I am*
Birth	**Birth**
<u>Painful emotions</u> *I have felt*	<u>Peaceful emotions</u> *As my authentic self, I feel*
<u>One issue</u> **START** → *How can I*	 ‾‾‾‾‾‾‾‾ Peace & joy rating 1–10 (low to high)

Can you conceive that your responses in the left column are not "bad" and those in the right column are not "good"? We need <u>all</u> parts of ourselves to create our wholeness.

Clear your mind by listing or journaling all your <u>worries, fears, and discouraging thoughts</u> about your question.

Allow your mind to become radiant by <u>brainstorming encouraging and hopeful ideas</u> about your question. What statements might a best friend, lover, or counselor offer?

CalmUp® Journey

Date: _____

Instructions: Begin in the bottom row. Enter your responses, moving up from left to right.

<u>Deep healing breath; conscious choices</u> **FINISH →** *(1) Today I choose to empower myself by* *(2) I share/serve by*	 _____ Peace & joy rating 1–10 (low to high)
## Spirit	## Spirit
<u>Illusions</u> (First clear your mind on the back of this page.) *I believed*	<u>Creative openings</u> *I open to*
## Society	## Society
<u>Poor choices impacting others</u> *My poor choices have included*	<u>Being of service</u> *With integrity, I will*
## Inward	## Inward
<u>Disheartening image</u> *I have pictured myself*	<u>Self-loving visualization</u> *Today I visualize myself*
## Live	## Live
<u>Disturbing physical symptoms</u> *I have experienced*	<u>Positive affirmation for your health</u> *I am*
## Birth	## Birth
<u>Painful emotions</u> *I have felt*	<u>Peaceful emotions</u> *As my authentic self, I feel*
<u>One issue</u> **START →** *How can I*	 _____ Peace & joy rating 1–10 (low to high)

*Can you conceive that your responses in the left column are not "bad" and those in the right column are not "good"? We need **all** parts of ourselves to create our wholeness.*

Clear your mind by listing or journaling all your <u>worries, fears, and discouraging thoughts</u> about your question.

Allow your mind to become radiant by <u>brainstorming encouraging and hopeful ideas</u> about your question. What statements might a best friend, lover, or counselor offer?

CalmUp® Journey

Date: _____

Instructions: Begin in the bottom row. Enter your responses, moving up from left to right.

Deep healing breath; conscious choices **FINISH** → *(1) Today I choose to empower myself by* *(2) I share/serve by*	 ‾‾‾‾‾‾ Peace & joy rating 1–10 (low to high)
Spirit	**Spirit**
Illusions (First clear your mind on the back of this page.) *I believed*	Creative openings *I open to*
Society	**Society**
Poor choices impacting others *My poor choices have included*	Being of service *With integrity, I will*
Inward	**Inward**
Disheartening image *I have pictured myself*	Self-loving visualization *Today I visualize myself*
Live	**Live**
Disturbing physical symptoms *I have experienced*	Positive affirmation for your health *I am*
Birth	**Birth**
Painful emotions *I have felt*	Peaceful emotions *As my authentic self, I feel*
One issue **START** → *How can I*	 ‾‾‾‾‾‾ Peace & joy rating 1–10 (low to high)

*Can you conceive that your responses in the left column are not "bad" and those in the right column are not "good"? We need **all** parts of ourselves to create our wholeness.*

Clear your mind by listing or journaling all your <u>worries, fears, and discouraging thoughts</u> about your question.

Allow your mind to become radiant by <u>brainstorming encouraging and hopeful ideas</u> about your question. What statements might a best friend, lover, or counselor offer?

CalmUp® Journey

Date: _____

Instructions: Begin in the bottom row. Enter your responses, moving up from left to right.

Deep healing breath; conscious choices **FINISH** → *(1) Today I choose to empower myself by* *(2) I share/serve by*	 ‾‾‾‾‾ Peace & joy rating 1–10 (low to high)
Spirit	**Spirit**
Illusions (First clear your mind on the back of this page.) *I believed*	Creative openings *I open to*
Society	**Society**
Poor choices impacting others *My poor choices have included*	Being of service *With integrity, I will*
Inward	**Inward**
Disheartening image *I have pictured myself*	Self-loving visualization *Today I visualize myself*
Live	**Live**
Disturbing physical symptoms *I have experienced*	Positive affirmation for your health *I am*
Birth	**Birth**
Painful emotions *I have felt*	Peaceful emotions *As my authentic self, I feel*
One issue **START** → *How can I*	 ‾‾‾‾‾ Peace & joy rating 1–10 (low to high)

Can you conceive that your responses in the left column are not "bad" and those in the right column are not "good"? We need <u>all</u> parts of ourselves to create our wholeness.

Clear your mind by listing or journaling all your <u>worries, fears, and discouraging thoughts</u> about your question.

Allow your mind to become radiant by <u>brainstorming encouraging and hopeful ideas</u> about your question. What statements might a best friend, lover, or counselor offer?

CalmUp® Journey

Date: _____

Instructions: Begin in the bottom row. Enter your responses, moving up from left to right.

Deep healing breath; conscious choices **FINISH →** *(1) Today I choose to empower myself by* *(2) I share/serve by*	 _____ Peace & joy rating 1–10 (low to high)
Spirit	**Spirit**
Illusions (First clear your mind on the back of this page.) *I believed*	Creative openings *I open to*
Society	**Society**
Poor choices impacting others *My poor choices have included*	Being of service *With integrity, I will*
Inward	**Inward**
Disheartening image *I have pictured myself*	Self-loving visualization *Today I visualize myself*
Live	**Live**
Disturbing physical symptoms *I have experienced*	Positive affirmation for your health *I am*
Birth	**Birth**
Painful emotions *I have felt*	Peaceful emotions *As my authentic self, I feel*
One issue **START →** *How can I*	 _____ Peace & joy rating 1–10 (low to high)

Can you conceive that your responses in the left column are not "bad" and those in the right column are not "good"? We need <u>all</u> parts of ourselves to create our wholeness.

www.drloriegose.com

Clear your mind by listing or journaling all your <u>worries, fears, and discouraging thoughts</u> about your question.

Allow your mind to become radiant by <u>brainstorming encouraging and hopeful ideas</u> about your question. What statements might a best friend, lover, or counselor offer?

CalmUp® Journey

Date: _____

Instructions: Begin in the bottom row. Enter your responses, moving up from left to right.

Deep healing breath; conscious choices **FINISH** → *(1) Today I choose to empower myself by* *(2) I share/serve by*	 ——— Peace & joy rating 1–10 (low to high)
Spirit	**Spirit**
Illusions (First clear your mind on the back of this page.) *I believed*	Creative openings *I open to*
Society	**Society**
Poor choices impacting others *My poor choices have included*	Being of service *With integrity, I will*
Inward	**Inward**
Disheartening image *I have pictured myself*	Self-loving visualization *Today I visualize myself*
Live	**Live**
Disturbing physical symptoms *I have experienced*	Positive affirmation for your health *I am*
Birth	**Birth**
Painful emotions *I have felt*	Peaceful emotions *As my authentic self, I feel*
One issue **START** → *How can I*	 ——— Peace & joy rating 1–10 (low to high)

Can you conceive that your responses in the left column are not "bad" and those in the right column are not "good"? We need <u>all</u> parts of ourselves to create our wholeness.

Clear your mind by listing or journaling all your <u>worries, fears, and discouraging thoughts</u> about your question.

Allow your mind to become radiant by <u>brainstorming encouraging and hopeful ideas</u> about your question. What statements might a best friend, lover, or counselor offer?

CalmUp® Journey

Date: _____

Instructions: Begin in the bottom row. Enter your responses, moving up from left to right.

<u>Deep healing breath; conscious choices</u> **FINISH** → *(1) Today I choose to empower myself by* *(2) I share/serve by*	 _____ Peace & joy rating 1–10 (low to high)
### Spirit	### Spirit
<u>Illusions</u> (First clear your mind on the back of this page.) *I believed*	<u>Creative openings</u> *I open to*
### Society	### Society
<u>Poor choices impacting others</u> *My poor choices have included*	<u>Being of service</u> *With integrity, I will*
### Inward	### Inward
<u>Disheartening image</u> *I have pictured myself*	<u>Self-loving visualization</u> *Today I visualize myself*
### Live	### Live
<u>Disturbing physical symptoms</u> *I have experienced*	<u>Positive affirmation for your health</u> *I am*
### Birth	### Birth
<u>Painful emotions</u> *I have felt*	<u>Peaceful emotions</u> *As my authentic self, I feel*
<u>One issue</u> **START** → *How can I*	 _____ Peace & joy rating 1–10 (low to high)

Can you conceive that your responses in the left column are not "bad" and those in the right column are not "good"? We need <u>all</u> parts of ourselves to create our wholeness.

Clear your mind by listing or journaling all your <u>worries, fears, and discouraging thoughts</u> about your question.

Allow your mind to become radiant by <u>brainstorming encouraging and hopeful ideas</u> about your question. What statements might a best friend, lover, or counselor offer?

CalmUp® Journey

Date: _____

Instructions: Begin in the bottom row. Enter your responses, moving up from left to right.

<u>Deep healing breath; conscious choices</u> **FINISH** → *(1) Today I choose to empower myself by* *(2) I share/serve by*	 _____ Peace & joy rating 1–10 (low to high)
Spirit	**Spirit**
<u>Illusions</u> (First clear your mind on the back of this page.) *I believed*	<u>Creative openings</u> *I open to*
Society	**Society**
<u>Poor choices impacting others</u> *My poor choices have included*	<u>Being of service</u> *With integrity, I will*
Inward	**Inward**
<u>Disheartening image</u> *I have pictured myself*	<u>Self-loving visualization</u> *Today I visualize myself*
Live	**Live**
<u>Disturbing physical symptoms</u> *I have experienced*	<u>Positive affirmation for your health</u> *I am*
Birth	**Birth**
<u>Painful emotions</u> *I have felt*	<u>Peaceful emotions</u> *As my authentic self, I feel*
<u>One issue</u> **START** → *How can I*	 _____ Peace & joy rating 1–10 (low to high)

*Can you conceive that your responses in the left column are not "bad" and those in the right column are not "good"? We need **all** parts of ourselves to create our wholeness.*

Clear your mind by listing or journaling all your <u>worries, fears, and discouraging thoughts</u> about your question.

Allow your mind to become radiant by <u>brainstorming encouraging and hopeful ideas</u> about your question. What statements might a best friend, lover, or counselor offer?

CalmUp® Journey

Date: _____

Instructions: Begin in the bottom row. Enter your responses, moving up from left to right.

<u>Deep healing breath; conscious choices</u> **FINISH** → *(1) Today I choose to empower myself by* *(2) I share/serve by*	 _____ Peace & joy rating 1–10 (low to high)
## Spirit	## Spirit
<u>Illusions</u> (First clear your mind on the back of this page.) *I believed*	<u>Creative openings</u> *I open to*
## Society	## Society
<u>Poor choices impacting others</u> *My poor choices have included*	<u>Being of service</u> *With integrity, I will*
## Inward	## Inward
<u>Disheartening image</u> *I have pictured myself*	<u>Self-loving visualization</u> *Today I visualize myself*
## Live	## Live
<u>Disturbing physical symptoms</u> *I have experienced*	<u>Positive affirmation for your health</u> *I am*
## Birth	## Birth
<u>Painful emotions</u> *I have felt*	<u>Peaceful emotions</u> *As my authentic self, I feel*
<u>One issue</u> **START** → *How can I*	 _____ Peace & joy rating 1–10 (low to high)

Can you conceive that your responses in the left column are not "bad" and those in the right column are not "good"? We need <u>all</u> parts of ourselves to create our wholeness.

Clear your mind by listing or journaling all your <u>worries, fears, and discouraging thoughts</u> about your question.

Allow your mind to become radiant by <u>brainstorming encouraging and hopeful ideas</u> about your question. What statements might a best friend, lover, or counselor offer?

CalmUp® Journey

Date: _____

Instructions: Begin in the bottom row. Enter your responses, moving up from left to right.

<u>Deep healing breath; conscious choices</u> **FINISH** → *(1) Today I choose to empower myself by* *(2) I share/serve by*	 _____ Peace & joy rating 1–10 (low to high)
Spirit	**Spirit**
<u>Illusions</u> (First clear your mind on the back of this page.) *I believed*	<u>Creative openings</u> *I open to*
Society	**Society**
<u>Poor choices impacting others</u> *My poor choices have included*	<u>Being of service</u> *With integrity, I will*
Inward	**Inward**
<u>Disheartening image</u> *I have pictured myself*	<u>Self-loving visualization</u> *Today I visualize myself*
Live	**Live**
<u>Disturbing physical symptoms</u> *I have experienced*	<u>Positive affirmation for your health</u> *I am*
Birth	**Birth**
<u>Painful emotions</u> *I have felt*	<u>Peaceful emotions</u> *As my authentic self, I feel*
<u>One issue</u> **START** → *How can I*	 _____ Peace & joy rating 1–10 (low to high)

Can you conceive that your responses in the left column are not "bad" and those in the right column are not "good"? We need __all__ parts of ourselves to create our wholeness.

Back Page

Clear your mind by listing or journaling all your <u>worries, fears, and discouraging thoughts</u> about your question.

Allow your mind to become radiant by <u>brainstorming encouraging and hopeful ideas</u> about your question. What statements might a best friend, lover, or counselor offer?

CalmUp® Journey

Date: _____

Instructions: Begin in the bottom row. Enter your responses, moving up from left to right.

<u>Deep healing breath; conscious choices</u> **FINISH** → *(1) Today I choose to empower myself by* *(2) I share/serve by*	 _____ Peace & joy rating 1–10 (low to high)
### Spirit	### Spirit
<u>Illusions</u> (First clear your mind on the back of this page.) *I believed*	<u>Creative openings</u> *I open to*
### Society	### Society
<u>Poor choices impacting others</u> *My poor choices have included*	<u>Being of service</u> *With integrity, I will*
### Inward	### Inward
<u>Disheartening image</u> *I have pictured myself*	<u>Self-loving visualization</u> *Today I visualize myself*
### Live	### Live
<u>Disturbing physical symptoms</u> *I have experienced*	<u>Positive affirmation for your health</u> *I am*
### Birth	### Birth
<u>Painful emotions</u> *I have felt*	<u>Peaceful emotions</u> *As my authentic self, I feel*
<u>One issue</u> **START** → *How can I*	 _____ Peace & joy rating 1–10 (low to high)

Can you conceive that your responses in the left column are not "bad" and those in the right column are not "good"? We need <u>all</u> parts of ourselves to create our wholeness.

Clear your mind by listing or journaling all your <u>worries, fears, and discouraging thoughts</u> about your question.

Allow your mind to become radiant by <u>brainstorming encouraging and hopeful ideas</u> about your question. What statements might a best friend, lover, or counselor offer?

CalmUp® Journey

Date: _____

Instructions: Begin in the bottom row. Enter your responses, moving up from left to right.

<u>Deep healing breath; conscious choices</u> **FINISH** → *(1) Today I choose to empower myself by* *(2) I share/serve by*	 _____ Peace & joy rating 1–10 (low to high)
### Spirit	### Spirit
<u>Illusions</u> (First clear your mind on the back of this page.) *I believed*	<u>Creative openings</u> *I open to*
### Society	### Society
<u>Poor choices impacting others</u> *My poor choices have included*	<u>Being of service</u> *With integrity, I will*
### Inward	### Inward
<u>Disheartening image</u> *I have pictured myself*	<u>Self-loving visualization</u> *Today I visualize myself*
### Live	### Live
<u>Disturbing physical symptoms</u> *I have experienced*	<u>Positive affirmation for your health</u> *I am*
### Birth	### Birth
<u>Painful emotions</u> *I have felt*	<u>Peaceful emotions</u> *As my authentic self, I feel*
<u>One issue</u> **START** → *How can I*	 _____ Peace & joy rating 1–10 (low to high)

*Can you conceive that your responses in the left column are not "bad" and those in the right column are not "good"? We need **all** parts of ourselves to create our wholeness.*

Clear your mind by listing or journaling all your <u>worries, fears, and discouraging thoughts</u> about your question.

Allow your mind to become radiant by <u>brainstorming encouraging and hopeful ideas</u> about your question. What statements might a best friend, lover, or counselor offer?

CalmUp® Journey

Date: _____

Instructions: Begin in the bottom row. Enter your responses, moving up from left to right.

<u>Deep healing breath; conscious choices</u> **FINISH** → *(1) Today I choose to empower myself by* *(2) I share/serve by*	 _____ Peace & joy rating 1–10 (low to high)
## Spirit	## Spirit
<u>Illusions</u> (First clear your mind on the back of this page.) *I believed*	<u>Creative openings</u> *I open to*
## Society	## Society
<u>Poor choices impacting others</u> *My poor choices have included*	<u>Being of service</u> *With integrity, I will*
## Inward	## Inward
<u>Disheartening image</u> *I have pictured myself*	<u>Self-loving visualization</u> *Today I visualize myself*
## Live	## Live
<u>Disturbing physical symptoms</u> *I have experienced*	<u>Positive affirmation for your health</u> *I am*
## Birth	## Birth
<u>Painful emotions</u> *I have felt*	<u>Peaceful emotions</u> *As my authentic self, I feel*
<u>One issue</u> **START** → *How can I*	 _____ Peace & joy rating 1–10 (low to high)

Can you conceive that your responses in the left column are not "bad" and those in the right column are not "good"? We need <u>all</u> parts of ourselves to create our wholeness.

Clear your mind by listing or journaling all your <u>worries, fears, and discouraging thoughts</u> about your question.

Allow your mind to become radiant by <u>brainstorming encouraging and hopeful ideas</u> about your question. What statements might a best friend, lover, or counselor offer?

CalmUp® Journey

Date: _____

Instructions: Begin in the bottom row. Enter your responses, moving up from left to right.

Deep healing breath; conscious choices **FINISH** → *(1) Today I choose to empower myself by* *(2) I share/serve by*	 ——— Peace & joy rating 1–10 (low to high)
Spirit	**Spirit**
Illusions (First clear your mind on the back of this page.) *I believed*	Creative openings *I open to*
Society	**Society**
Poor choices impacting others *My poor choices have included*	Being of service *With integrity, I will*
Inward	**Inward**
Disheartening image *I have pictured myself*	Self-loving visualization *Today I visualize myself*
Live	**Live**
Disturbing physical symptoms *I have experienced*	Positive affirmation for your health *I am*
Birth	**Birth**
Painful emotions *I have felt*	Peaceful emotions *As my authentic self, I feel*
One issue **START** → *How can I*	 ——— Peace & joy rating 1–10 (low to high)

Can you conceive that your responses in the left column are not "bad" and those in the right column are not "good"? We need <u>all</u> parts of ourselves to create our wholeness.

www.drloriegose.com

Clear your mind by listing or journaling all your <u>worries, fears, and discouraging thoughts</u> about your question.

Allow your mind to become radiant by <u>brainstorming encouraging and hopeful ideas</u> about your question. What statements might a best friend, lover, or counselor offer?

CalmUp® Journey

Date: _____

Instructions: Begin in the bottom row. Enter your responses, moving up from left to right.

<u>Deep healing breath; conscious choices</u> **FINISH** → *(1) Today I choose to empower myself by* *(2) I share/serve by*	 _____ Peace & joy rating 1–10 (low to high)
## Spirit	## Spirit
<u>Illusions</u> (First clear your mind on the back of this page.) *I believed*	<u>Creative openings</u> *I open to*
## Society	## Society
<u>Poor choices impacting others</u> *My poor choices have included*	<u>Being of service</u> *With integrity, I will*
## Inward	## Inward
<u>Disheartening image</u> *I have pictured myself*	<u>Self-loving visualization</u> *Today I visualize myself*
## Live	## Live
<u>Disturbing physical symptoms</u> *I have experienced*	<u>Positive affirmation for your health</u> *I am*
## Birth	## Birth
<u>Painful emotions</u> *I have felt*	<u>Peaceful emotions</u> *As my authentic self, I feel*
<u>One issue</u> **START** → *How can I*	 _____ Peace & joy rating 1–10 (low to high)

Can you conceive that your responses in the left column are not "bad" and those in the right column are not "good"? We need <u>all</u> parts of ourselves to create our wholeness.

Clear your mind by listing or journaling all your <u>worries, fears, and discouraging thoughts</u> about your question.

Allow your mind to become radiant by <u>brainstorming encouraging and hopeful ideas</u> about your question. What statements might a best friend, lover, or counselor offer?

CalmUp® Journey

Date: _____

Instructions: Begin in the bottom row. Enter your responses, moving up from left to right.

Deep healing breath; conscious choices **FINISH** → *(1) Today I choose to empower myself by* *(2) I share/serve by*	 _____ Peace & joy rating 1–10 (low to high)
Spirit	**Spirit**
Illusions (First clear your mind on the back of this page.) *I believed*	Creative openings *I open to*
Society	**Society**
Poor choices impacting others *My poor choices have included*	Being of service *With integrity, I will*
Inward	**Inward**
Disheartening image *I have pictured myself*	Self-loving visualization *Today I visualize myself*
Live	**Live**
Disturbing physical symptoms *I have experienced*	Positive affirmation for your health *I am*
Birth	**Birth**
Painful emotions *I have felt*	Peaceful emotions *As my authentic self, I feel*
One issue **START** → *How can I*	 _____ Peace & joy rating 1–10 (low to high)

Can you conceive that your responses in the left column are not "bad" and those in the right column are not "good"? We need __all__ parts of ourselves to create our wholeness.

Clear your mind by listing or journaling all your <u>worries, fears, and discouraging thoughts</u> about your question.

Allow your mind to become radiant by <u>brainstorming encouraging and hopeful ideas</u> about your question. What statements might a best friend, lover, or counselor offer?

CalmUp® Journey

Date: _____

Instructions: Begin in the bottom row. Enter your responses, moving up from left to right.

<u>Deep healing breath; conscious choices</u> **FINISH** → *(1) Today I choose to empower myself by* *(2) I share/serve by*	 _____ Peace & joy rating 1–10 (low to high)
Spirit	**Spirit**
<u>Illusions</u> (First clear your mind on the back of this page.) *I believed*	<u>Creative openings</u> *I open to*
Society	**Society**
<u>Poor choices impacting others</u> *My poor choices have included*	<u>Being of service</u> *With integrity, I will*
Inward	**Inward**
<u>Disheartening image</u> *I have pictured myself*	<u>Self-loving visualization</u> *Today I visualize myself*
Live	**Live**
<u>Disturbing physical symptoms</u> *I have experienced*	<u>Positive affirmation for your health</u> *I am*
Birth	**Birth**
<u>Painful emotions</u> *I have felt*	<u>Peaceful emotions</u> *As my authentic self, I feel*
<u>One issue</u> **START** → *How can I*	 _____ Peace & joy rating 1–10 (low to high)

Can you conceive that your responses in the left column are not "bad" and those in the right column are not "good"? We need <u>all</u> parts of ourselves to create our wholeness.

Clear your mind by listing or journaling all your <u>worries, fears, and discouraging thoughts</u> about your question.

Allow your mind to become radiant by <u>brainstorming encouraging and hopeful ideas</u> about your question. What statements might a best friend, lover, or counselor offer?

CalmUp® Journey

Date: _____

Instructions: Begin in the bottom row. Enter your responses, moving up from left to right.

Deep healing breath; conscious choices **FINISH** → *(1) Today I choose to empower myself by* *(2) I share/serve by*	 _____ Peace & joy rating 1–10 (low to high)
Spirit	**Spirit**
Illusions (First clear your mind on the back of this page.) *I believed*	Creative openings *I open to*
Society	**Society**
Poor choices impacting others *My poor choices have included*	Being of service *With integrity, I will*
Inward	**Inward**
Disheartening image *I have pictured myself*	Self-loving visualization *Today I visualize myself*
Live	**Live**
Disturbing physical symptoms *I have experienced*	Positive affirmation for your health *I am*
Birth	**Birth**
Painful emotions *I have felt*	Peaceful emotions *As my authentic self, I feel*
One issue **START** → *How can I*	 _____ Peace & joy rating 1–10 (low to high)

Can you conceive that your responses in the left column are not "bad" and those in the right column are not "good"? We need all parts of ourselves to create our wholeness.

Clear your mind by listing or journaling all your <u>worries, fears, and discouraging thoughts</u> about your question.

Allow your mind to become radiant by <u>brainstorming encouraging and hopeful ideas</u> about your question. What statements might a best friend, lover, or counselor offer?

CalmUp® Journey

Date: _____

Instructions: Begin in the bottom row. Enter your responses, moving up from left to right.

<u>Deep healing breath; conscious choices</u> **FINISH** → *(1) Today I choose to empower myself by* *(2) I share/serve by*	 _____ Peace & joy rating 1–10 (low to high)
### Spirit	### Spirit
<u>Illusions</u> (First clear your mind on the back of this page.) *I believed*	<u>Creative openings</u> *I open to*
### Society	### Society
<u>Poor choices impacting others</u> *My poor choices have included*	<u>Being of service</u> *With integrity, I will*
### Inward	### Inward
<u>Disheartening image</u> *I have pictured myself*	<u>Self-loving visualization</u> *Today I visualize myself*
### Live	### Live
<u>Disturbing physical symptoms</u> *I have experienced*	<u>Positive affirmation for your health</u> *I am*
### Birth	### Birth
<u>Painful emotions</u> *I have felt*	<u>Peaceful emotions</u> *As my authentic self, I feel*
<u>One issue</u> **START** → *How can I*	 _____ Peace & joy rating 1–10 (low to high)

Can you conceive that your responses in the left column are not "bad" and those in the right column are not "good"? We need <u>all</u> parts of ourselves to create our wholeness.

Back Page

Clear your mind by listing or journaling all your <u>worries, fears, and discouraging thoughts</u> about your question.

Allow your mind to become radiant by <u>brainstorming encouraging and hopeful ideas</u> about your question. What statements might a best friend, lover, or counselor offer?

CalmUp® Journey

Date: _____

Instructions: Begin in the bottom row. Enter your responses, moving up from left to right.

Deep healing breath; conscious choices **FINISH** → *(1) Today I choose to empower myself by* *(2) I share/serve by*	 _____ Peace & joy rating 1–10 (low to high)
Spirit	**Spirit**
Illusions (First clear your mind on the back of this page.) *I believed*	Creative openings *I open to*
Society	**Society**
Poor choices impacting others *My poor choices have included*	Being of service *With integrity, I will*
Inward	**Inward**
Disheartening image *I have pictured myself*	Self-loving visualization *Today I visualize myself*
Live	**Live**
Disturbing physical symptoms *I have experienced*	Positive affirmation for your health *I am*
Birth	**Birth**
Painful emotions *I have felt*	Peaceful emotions *As my authentic self, I feel*
One issue **START** → *How can I*	 _____ Peace & joy rating 1–10 (low to high)

Can you conceive that your responses in the left column are not "bad" and those in the right column are not "good"? We need all parts of ourselves to create our wholeness.

www.drloriegose.com

Clear your mind by listing or journaling all your <u>worries, fears, and discouraging thoughts</u> about your question.

Allow your mind to become radiant by <u>brainstorming encouraging and hopeful ideas</u> about your question. What statements might a best friend, lover, or counselor offer?

CalmUp® Journey

Date: _____

Instructions: Begin in the bottom row. Enter your responses, moving up from left to right.

<u>Deep healing breath; conscious choices</u> **FINISH** → *(1) Today I choose to empower myself by* *(2) I share/serve by*	 _____ Peace & joy rating 1–10 (low to high)
Spirit	**Spirit**
<u>Illusions</u> (First clear your mind on the back of this page.) *I believed*	<u>Creative openings</u> *I open to*
Society	**Society**
<u>Poor choices impacting others</u> *My poor choices have included*	<u>Being of service</u> *With integrity, I will*
Inward	**Inward**
<u>Disheartening image</u> *I have pictured myself*	<u>Self-loving visualization</u> *Today I visualize myself*
Live	**Live**
<u>Disturbing physical symptoms</u> *I have experienced*	<u>Positive affirmation for your health</u> *I am*
Birth	**Birth**
<u>Painful emotions</u> *I have felt*	<u>Peaceful emotions</u> *As my authentic self, I feel*
<u>One issue</u> **START** → *How can I*	 _____ Peace & joy rating 1–10 (low to high)

Can you conceive that your responses in the left column are not "bad" and those in the right column are not "good"? We need <u>all</u> parts of ourselves to create our wholeness.

Clear your mind by listing or journaling all your <u>worries, fears, and discouraging thoughts</u> about your question.

Allow your mind to become radiant by <u>brainstorming encouraging and hopeful ideas</u> about your question. What statements might a best friend, lover, or counselor offer?

CalmUp® Journey

Date: _____

Instructions: Begin in the bottom row. Enter your responses, moving up from left to right.

Deep healing breath; conscious choices **FINISH** → *(1) Today I choose to empower myself by* *(2) I share/serve by*	 _____ Peace & joy rating 1–10 (low to high)
## Spirit	## Spirit
Illusions (First clear your mind on the back of this page.) *I believed*	Creative openings *I open to*
## Society	## Society
Poor choices impacting others *My poor choices have included*	Being of service *With integrity, I will*
## Inward	## Inward
Disheartening image *I have pictured myself*	Self-loving visualization *Today I visualize myself*
## Live	## Live
Disturbing physical symptoms *I have experienced*	Positive affirmation for your health *I am*
## Birth	## Birth
Painful emotions *I have felt*	Peaceful emotions *As my authentic self, I feel*
One issue **START** → *How can I*	 _____ Peace & joy rating 1–10 (low to high)

Can you conceive that your responses in the left column are not "bad" and those in the right column are not "good"? We need all parts of ourselves to create our wholeness.

Clear your mind by listing or journaling all your <u>worries, fears, and discouraging thoughts</u> about your question.

Allow your mind to become radiant by <u>brainstorming encouraging and hopeful ideas</u> about your question. What statements might a best friend, lover, or counselor offer?

CalmUp® Journey

Date: _____

Instructions: Begin in the bottom row. Enter your responses, moving up from left to right.

Deep healing breath; conscious choices **FINISH** → *(1) Today I choose to empower myself by* *(2) I share/serve by*	 ‾‾‾‾‾‾ Peace & joy rating 1–10 (low to high)
Spirit	**Spirit**
Illusions (First clear your mind on the back of this page.) *I believed*	Creative openings *I open to*
Society	**Society**
Poor choices impacting others *My poor choices have included*	Being of service *With integrity, I will*
Inward	**Inward**
Disheartening image *I have pictured myself*	Self-loving visualization *Today I visualize myself*
Live	**Live**
Disturbing physical symptoms *I have experienced*	Positive affirmation for your health *I am*
Birth	**Birth**
Painful emotions *I have felt*	Peaceful emotions *As my authentic self, I feel*
One issue **START** → *How can I*	 ‾‾‾‾‾‾ Peace & joy rating 1–10 (low to high)

Can you conceive that your responses in the left column are not "bad" and those in the right column are not "good"? We need __all__ parts of ourselves to create our wholeness.

Clear your mind by listing or journaling all your <u>worries, fears, and discouraging thoughts</u> about your question.

Allow your mind to become radiant by <u>brainstorming encouraging and hopeful ideas</u> about your question. What statements might a best friend, lover, or counselor offer?

CalmUp® Journey

Date: _____

Instructions: Begin in the bottom row. Enter your responses, moving up from left to right.

Deep healing breath; conscious choices **FINISH** → *(1) Today I choose to empower myself by* *(2) I share/serve by*	 _____ Peace & joy rating 1–10 (low to high)
### Spirit Illusions (First clear your mind on the back of this page.) *I believed*	### Spirit Creative openings *I open to*
### Society Poor choices impacting others *My poor choices have included*	### Society Being of service *With integrity, I will*
### Inward Disheartening image *I have pictured myself*	### Inward Self-loving visualization *Today I visualize myself*
### Live Disturbing physical symptoms *I have experienced*	### Live Positive affirmation for your health *I am*
### Birth Painful emotions *I have felt*	### Birth Peaceful emotions *As my authentic self, I feel*
One issue **START** → *How can I*	 _____ Peace & joy rating 1–10 (low to high)

Can you conceive that your responses in the left column are not "bad" and those in the
*right column are not "good"? We need **all** parts of ourselves to create our wholeness.*

Clear your mind by listing or journaling all your <u>worries, fears, and discouraging thoughts</u> about your question.

Allow your mind to become radiant by <u>brainstorming encouraging and hopeful ideas</u> about your question. What statements might a best friend, lover, or counselor offer?

CalmUp® Journey

Date: _____

Instructions: Begin in the bottom row. Enter your responses, moving up from left to right.

<u>Deep healing breath; conscious choices</u> **FINISH** → *(1) Today I choose to empower myself by* *(2) I share/serve by*	 ———————— Peace & joy rating 1–10 (low to high)
### Spirit	### Spirit
<u>Illusions</u> (First clear your mind on the back of this page.) *I believed*	<u>Creative openings</u> *I open to*
### Society	### Society
<u>Poor choices impacting others</u> *My poor choices have included*	<u>Being of service</u> *With integrity, I will*
### Inward	### Inward
<u>Disheartening image</u> *I have pictured myself*	<u>Self-loving visualization</u> *Today I visualize myself*
### Live	### Live
<u>Disturbing physical symptoms</u> *I have experienced*	<u>Positive affirmation for your health</u> *I am*
### Birth	### Birth
<u>Painful emotions</u> *I have felt*	<u>Peaceful emotions</u> *As my authentic self, I feel*
<u>One issue</u> **START** → *How can I*	 ———————— Peace & joy rating 1–10 (low to high)

Can you conceive that your responses in the left column are not "bad" and those in the right column are not "good"? We need <u>all</u> parts of ourselves to create our wholeness.

Clear your mind by listing or journaling all your <u>worries, fears, and discouraging thoughts</u> about your question.

Allow your mind to become radiant by <u>brainstorming encouraging and hopeful ideas</u> about your question. What statements might a best friend, lover, or counselor offer?

CalmUp® Journey

Date: _____

Instructions: Begin in the bottom row. Enter your responses, moving up from left to right.

Deep healing breath; conscious choices **FINISH** → *(1) Today I choose to empower myself by* *(2) I share/serve by*	 _____ Peace & joy rating 1–10 (low to high)
### Spirit	### Spirit
Illusions (First clear your mind on the back of this page.) *I believed*	Creative openings *I open to*
### Society	### Society
Poor choices impacting others *My poor choices have included*	Being of service *With integrity, I will*
### Inward	### Inward
Disheartening image *I have pictured myself*	Self-loving visualization *Today I visualize myself*
### Live	### Live
Disturbing physical symptoms *I have experienced*	Positive affirmation for your health *I am*
### Birth	### Birth
Painful emotions *I have felt*	Peaceful emotions *As my authentic self, I feel*
One issue **START** → *How can I*	 _____ Peace & joy rating 1–10 (low to high)

Can you conceive that your responses in the left column are not "bad" and those in the right column are not "good"? We need all parts of ourselves to create our wholeness.

www.drloriegose.com

Clear your mind by listing or journaling all your <u>worries, fears, and discouraging thoughts</u> about your question.

Allow your mind to become radiant by <u>brainstorming encouraging and hopeful ideas</u> about your question. What statements might a best friend, lover, or counselor offer?

CalmUp® Journey

Date: _____

Instructions: Begin in the bottom row. Enter your responses, moving up from left to right.

<u>Deep healing breath; conscious choices</u> **FINISH** → *(1) Today I choose to empower myself by* *(2) I share/serve by*	 _____ Peace & joy rating 1–10 (low to high)
### Spirit	### Spirit
<u>Illusions</u> (First clear your mind on the back of this page.) *I believed*	<u>Creative openings</u> *I open to*
### Society	### Society
<u>Poor choices impacting others</u> *My poor choices have included*	<u>Being of service</u> *With integrity, I will*
### Inward	### Inward
<u>Disheartening image</u> *I have pictured myself*	<u>Self-loving visualization</u> *Today I visualize myself*
### Live	### Live
<u>Disturbing physical symptoms</u> *I have experienced*	<u>Positive affirmation for your health</u> *I am*
### Birth	### Birth
<u>Painful emotions</u> *I have felt*	<u>Peaceful emotions</u> *As my authentic self, I feel*
<u>One issue</u> **START** → *How can I*	 _____ Peace & joy rating 1–10 (low to high)

Can you conceive that your responses in the left column are not "bad" and those in the right column are not "good"? We need <u>all</u> parts of ourselves to create our wholeness.

Clear your mind by listing or journaling all your <u>worries, fears, and discouraging thoughts</u> about your question.

Allow your mind to become radiant by <u>brainstorming encouraging and hopeful ideas</u> about your question. What statements might a best friend, lover, or counselor offer?

CalmUp® Journey

Date: _____

Instructions: Begin in the bottom row. Enter your responses, moving up from left to right.

Deep healing breath; conscious choices **FINISH** → *(1) Today I choose to empower myself by* *(2) I share/serve by*	 _____ Peace & joy rating 1–10 (low to high)
Spirit	**Spirit**
Illusions (First clear your mind on the back of this page.) *I believed*	Creative openings *I open to*
Society	**Society**
Poor choices impacting others *My poor choices have included*	Being of service *With integrity, I will*
Inward	**Inward**
Disheartening image *I have pictured myself*	Self-loving visualization *Today I visualize myself*
Live	**Live**
Disturbing physical symptoms *I have experienced*	Positive affirmation for your health *I am*
Birth	**Birth**
Painful emotions *I have felt*	Peaceful emotions *As my authentic self, I feel*
One issue **START** → *How can I*	 _____ Peace & joy rating 1–10 (low to high)

Can you conceive that your responses in the left column are not "bad" and those in the right column are not "good"? We need all parts of ourselves to create our wholeness.

Clear your mind by listing or journaling all your <u>worries, fears, and discouraging thoughts</u> about your question.

Allow your mind to become radiant by <u>brainstorming encouraging and hopeful ideas</u> about your question. What statements might a best friend, lover, or counselor offer?

CalmUp® Journey

Date: _____

Instructions: Begin in the bottom row. Enter your responses, moving up from left to right.

<u>Deep healing breath; conscious choices</u> **FINISH** → *(1) Today I choose to empower myself by* *(2) I share/serve by*	 ———— Peace & joy rating 1–10 (low to high)
Spirit	**Spirit**
<u>Illusions</u> (First clear your mind on the back of this page.) *I believed*	<u>Creative openings</u> *I open to*
Society	**Society**
<u>Poor choices impacting others</u> *My poor choices have included*	<u>Being of service</u> *With integrity, I will*
Inward	**Inward**
<u>Disheartening image</u> *I have pictured myself*	<u>Self-loving visualization</u> *Today I visualize myself*
Live	**Live**
<u>Disturbing physical symptoms</u> *I have experienced*	<u>Positive affirmation for your health</u> *I am*
Birth	**Birth**
<u>Painful emotions</u> *I have felt*	<u>Peaceful emotions</u> *As my authentic self, I feel*
<u>One issue</u> **START** → *How can I*	 ———— Peace & joy rating 1–10 (low to high)

*Can you conceive that your responses in the left column are not "bad" and those in the right column are not "good"? We need **all** parts of ourselves to create our wholeness.*

Clear your mind by listing or journaling all your <u>worries, fears, and discouraging thoughts</u> about your question.

Allow your mind to become radiant by <u>brainstorming encouraging and hopeful ideas</u> about your question. What statements might a best friend, lover, or counselor offer?

CalmUp® Journey

Date: _____

Instructions: Begin in the bottom row. Enter your responses, moving up from left to right.

<u>Deep healing breath; conscious choices</u> **FINISH →** *(1) Today I choose to empower myself by* *(2) I share/serve by*	 _____ Peace & joy rating 1–10 (low to high)
### Spirit	### Spirit
<u>Illusions</u> (First clear your mind on the back of this page.) *I believed*	<u>Creative openings</u> *I open to*
### Society	### Society
<u>Poor choices impacting others</u> *My poor choices have included*	<u>Being of service</u> *With integrity, I will*
### Inward	### Inward
<u>Disheartening image</u> *I have pictured myself*	<u>Self-loving visualization</u> *Today I visualize myself*
### Live	### Live
<u>Disturbing physical symptoms</u> *I have experienced*	<u>Positive affirmation for your health</u> *I am*
### Birth	### Birth
<u>Painful emotions</u> *I have felt*	<u>Peaceful emotions</u> *As my authentic self, I feel*
<u>One issue</u> **START →** *How can I*	 _____ Peace & joy rating 1–10 (low to high)

Can you conceive that your responses in the left column are not "bad" and those in the right column are not "good"? We need <u>all</u> parts of ourselves to create our wholeness.

Clear your mind by listing or journaling all your <u>worries, fears, and discouraging thoughts</u> about your question.

Allow your mind to become radiant by <u>brainstorming encouraging and hopeful ideas</u> about your question. What statements might a best friend, lover, or counselor offer?

CalmUp® Journey

Date: _____

Instructions: Begin in the bottom row. Enter your responses, moving up from left to right.

Deep healing breath; conscious choices **FINISH** → *(1) Today I choose to empower myself by* *(2) I share/serve by*	 _____ Peace & joy rating 1–10 (low to high)
## Spirit	## Spirit
Illusions (First clear your mind on the back of this page.) *I believed*	Creative openings *I open to*
## Society	## Society
Poor choices impacting others *My poor choices have included*	Being of service *With integrity, I will*
## Inward	## Inward
Disheartening image *I have pictured myself*	Self-loving visualization *Today I visualize myself*
## Live	## Live
Disturbing physical symptoms *I have experienced*	Positive affirmation for your health *I am*
## Birth	## Birth
Painful emotions *I have felt*	Peaceful emotions *As my authentic self, I feel*
One issue **START** → *How can I*	 _____ Peace & joy rating 1–10 (low to high)

Can you conceive that your responses in the left column are not "bad" and those in the right column are not "good"? We need __all__ parts of ourselves to create our wholeness.

Clear your mind by listing or journaling all your <u>worries, fears, and discouraging thoughts</u> about your question.

Allow your mind to become radiant by <u>brainstorming encouraging and hopeful ideas</u> about your question. What statements might a best friend, lover, or counselor offer?

CalmUp® Journey

Date: _____

Instructions: Begin in the bottom row. Enter your responses, moving up from left to right.

<u>Deep healing breath; conscious choices</u> **FINISH** → *(1) Today I choose to empower myself by* *(2) I share/serve by*	 ‾‾‾‾‾‾‾ Peace & joy rating 1–10 (low to high)
## Spirit	## Spirit
<u>Illusions</u> (First clear your mind on the back of this page.) *I believed*	<u>Creative openings</u> *I open to*
## Society	## Society
<u>Poor choices impacting others</u> *My poor choices have included*	<u>Being of service</u> *With integrity, I will*
## Inward	## Inward
<u>Disheartening image</u> *I have pictured myself*	<u>Self-loving visualization</u> *Today I visualize myself*
## Live	## Live
<u>Disturbing physical symptoms</u> *I have experienced*	<u>Positive affirmation for your health</u> *I am*
## Birth	## Birth
<u>Painful emotions</u> *I have felt*	<u>Peaceful emotions</u> *As my authentic self, I feel*
<u>One issue</u> **START** → *How can I*	 ‾‾‾‾‾‾‾ Peace & joy rating 1–10 (low to high)

Can you conceive that your responses in the left column are not "bad" and those in the right column are not "good"? We need <u>all</u> parts of ourselves to create our wholeness.

Clear your mind by listing or journaling all your <u>worries, fears, and discouraging thoughts</u> about your question.

Allow your mind to become radiant by <u>brainstorming encouraging and hopeful ideas</u> about your question. What statements might a best friend, lover, or counselor offer?

CalmUp® Journey

Date: _____

Instructions: Begin in the bottom row. Enter your responses, moving up from left to right.

Deep healing breath; conscious choices **FINISH** → *(1) Today I choose to empower myself by* *(2) I share/serve by*	 _____ Peace & joy rating 1–10 (low to high)
Spirit	**Spirit**
Illusions (First clear your mind on the back of this page.) *I believed*	Creative openings *I open to*
Society	**Society**
Poor choices impacting others *My poor choices have included*	Being of service *With integrity, I will*
Inward	**Inward**
Disheartening image *I have pictured myself*	Self-loving visualization *Today I visualize myself*
Live	**Live**
Disturbing physical symptoms *I have experienced*	Positive affirmation for your health *I am*
Birth	**Birth**
Painful emotions *I have felt*	Peaceful emotions *As my authentic self, I feel*
One issue **START** → *How can I*	 _____ Peace & joy rating 1–10 (low to high)

Can you conceive that your responses in the left column are not "bad" and those in the right column are not "good"? We need <u>all</u> parts of ourselves to create our wholeness.

Clear your mind by listing or journaling all your <u>worries, fears, and discouraging thoughts</u> about your question.

Allow your mind to become radiant by <u>brainstorming encouraging and hopeful ideas</u> about your question. What statements might a best friend, lover, or counselor offer?

CalmUp® Journey

Date: _____

Instructions: Begin in the bottom row. Enter your responses, moving up from left to right.

<u>Deep healing breath; conscious choices</u> **FINISH** → *(1) Today I choose to empower myself by* *(2) I share/serve by*	 ‾‾‾‾‾‾‾ Peace & joy rating 1–10 (low to high)
Spirit	**Spirit**
<u>Illusions</u> (First clear your mind on the back of this page.) *I believed*	<u>Creative openings</u> *I open to*
Society	**Society**
<u>Poor choices impacting others</u> *My poor choices have included*	<u>Being of service</u> *With integrity, I will*
Inward	**Inward**
<u>Disheartening image</u> *I have pictured myself*	<u>Self-loving visualization</u> *Today I visualize myself*
Live	**Live**
<u>Disturbing physical symptoms</u> *I have experienced*	<u>Positive affirmation for your health</u> *I am*
Birth	**Birth**
<u>Painful emotions</u> *I have felt*	<u>Peaceful emotions</u> *As my authentic self, I feel*
<u>One issue</u> **START** → *How can I*	 ‾‾‾‾‾‾‾ Peace & joy rating 1–10 (low to high)

Can you conceive that your responses in the left column are not "bad" and those in the right column are not "good"? We need all parts of ourselves to create our wholeness.

Clear your mind by listing or journaling all your <u>worries, fears, and discouraging thoughts</u> about your question.

Allow your mind to become radiant by <u>brainstorming encouraging and hopeful ideas</u> about your question. What statements might a best friend, lover, or counselor offer?

CalmUp® Journey

Date: _____

Instructions: Begin in the bottom row. Enter your responses, moving up from left to right.

<u>Deep healing breath; conscious choices</u> **FINISH** → *(1) Today I choose to empower myself by* *(2) I share/serve by*	 _____ Peace & joy rating 1–10 (low to high)
Spirit	**Spirit**
<u>Illusions</u> (First clear your mind on the back of this page.) *I believed*	<u>Creative openings</u> *I open to*
Society	**Society**
<u>Poor choices impacting others</u> *My poor choices have included*	<u>Being of service</u> *With integrity, I will*
Inward	**Inward**
<u>Disheartening image</u> *I have pictured myself*	<u>Self-loving visualization</u> *Today I visualize myself*
Live	**Live**
<u>Disturbing physical symptoms</u> *I have experienced*	<u>Positive affirmation for your health</u> *I am*
Birth	**Birth**
<u>Painful emotions</u> *I have felt*	<u>Peaceful emotions</u> *As my authentic self, I feel*
<u>One issue</u> **START** → *How can I*	 _____ Peace & joy rating 1–10 (low to high)

Can you conceive that your responses in the left column are not "bad" and those in the right column are not "good"? We need <u>all</u> parts of ourselves to create our wholeness.

Clear your mind by listing or journaling all your <u>worries, fears, and discouraging thoughts</u> about your question.

Allow your mind to become radiant by <u>brainstorming encouraging and hopeful ideas</u> about your question. What statements might a best friend, lover, or counselor offer?

CalmUp® Journey

Date: _____

Instructions: Begin in the bottom row. Enter your responses, moving up from left to right.

<u>Deep healing breath; conscious choices</u> **FINISH** → *(1) Today I choose to empower myself by* *(2) I share/serve by*	 ———— Peace & joy rating 1–10 (low to high)
Spirit	**Spirit**
<u>Illusions</u> (First clear your mind on the back of this page.) *I believed*	<u>Creative openings</u> *I open to*
Society	**Society**
<u>Poor choices impacting others</u> *My poor choices have included*	<u>Being of service</u> *With integrity, I will*
Inward	**Inward**
<u>Disheartening image</u> *I have pictured myself*	<u>Self-loving visualization</u> *Today I visualize myself*
Live	**Live**
<u>Disturbing physical symptoms</u> *I have experienced*	<u>Positive affirmation for your health</u> *I am*
Birth	**Birth**
<u>Painful emotions</u> *I have felt*	<u>Peaceful emotions</u> *As my authentic self, I feel*
<u>One issue</u> **START** → *How can I*	 ———— Peace & joy rating 1–10 (low to high)

Can you conceive that your responses in the left column are not "bad" and those in the right column are not "good"? We need <u>all</u> parts of ourselves to create our wholeness.

Clear your mind by listing or journaling all your <u>worries, fears, and discouraging thoughts</u> about your question.

Allow your mind to become radiant by <u>brainstorming encouraging and hopeful ideas</u> about your question. What statements might a best friend, lover, or counselor offer?

CalmUp® Journey

Date: _____

Instructions: Begin in the bottom row. Enter your responses, moving up from left to right.

Deep healing breath; conscious choices **FINISH** → *(1) Today I choose to empower myself by* *(2) I share/serve by*	_____ Peace & joy rating 1–10 (low to high)
Spirit	**Spirit**
Illusions (First clear your mind on the back of this page.) *I believed*	Creative openings *I open to*
Society	**Society**
Poor choices impacting others *My poor choices have included*	Being of service *With integrity, I will*
Inward	**Inward**
Disheartening image *I have pictured myself*	Self-loving visualization *Today I visualize myself*
Live	**Live**
Disturbing physical symptoms *I have experienced*	Positive affirmation for your health *I am*
Birth	**Birth**
Painful emotions *I have felt*	Peaceful emotions *As my authentic self, I feel*
One issue **START** → *How can I*	_____ Peace & joy rating 1–10 (low to high)

Can you conceive that your responses in the left column are not "bad" and those in the right column are not "good"? We need __all__ parts of ourselves to create our wholeness.

Clear your mind by listing or journaling all your <u>worries, fears, and discouraging thoughts</u> about your question.

Allow your mind to become radiant by <u>brainstorming encouraging and hopeful ideas</u> about your question. What statements might a best friend, lover, or counselor offer?

CalmUp® Journey

Date: _____

Instructions: Begin in the bottom row. Enter your responses, moving up from left to right.

<u>Deep healing breath; conscious choices</u> **FINISH** → *(1) Today I choose to empower myself by* *(2) I share/serve by*	 _____ Peace & joy rating 1–10 (low to high)
Spirit	**Spirit**
<u>Illusions</u> (First clear your mind on the back of this page.) *I believed*	<u>Creative openings</u> *I open to*
Society	**Society**
<u>Poor choices impacting others</u> *My poor choices have included*	<u>Being of service</u> *With integrity, I will*
Inward	**Inward**
<u>Disheartening image</u> *I have pictured myself*	<u>Self-loving visualization</u> *Today I visualize myself*
Live	**Live**
<u>Disturbing physical symptoms</u> *I have experienced*	<u>Positive affirmation for your health</u> *I am*
Birth	**Birth**
<u>Painful emotions</u> *I have felt*	<u>Peaceful emotions</u> *As my authentic self, I feel*
<u>One issue</u> **START** → *How can I*	 _____ Peace & joy rating 1–10 (low to high)

*Can you conceive that your responses in the left column are not "bad" and those in the right column are not "good"? We need **all** parts of ourselves to create our wholeness.*

Clear your mind by listing or journaling all your <u>worries, fears, and discouraging thoughts</u> about your question.

Allow your mind to become radiant by <u>brainstorming encouraging and hopeful ideas</u> about your question. What statements might a best friend, lover, or counselor offer?

CalmUp® Journey

Date: _____

Instructions: Begin in the bottom row. Enter your responses, moving up from left to right.

Deep healing breath; conscious choices **FINISH** → *(1) Today I choose to empower myself by* *(2) I share/serve by*	 _____ Peace & joy rating 1–10 (low to high)
Spirit	**Spirit**
Illusions (First clear your mind on the back of this page.) *I believed*	Creative openings *I open to*
Society	**Society**
Poor choices impacting others *My poor choices have included*	Being of service *With integrity, I will*
Inward	**Inward**
Disheartening image *I have pictured myself*	Self-loving visualization *Today I visualize myself*
Live	**Live**
Disturbing physical symptoms *I have experienced*	Positive affirmation for your health *I am*
Birth	**Birth**
Painful emotions *I have felt*	Peaceful emotions *As my authentic self, I feel*
One issue **START** → *How can I*	 _____ Peace & joy rating 1–10 (low to high)

Can you conceive that your responses in the left column are not "bad" and those in the right column are not "good"? We need __all__ parts of ourselves to create our wholeness.

Clear your mind by listing or journaling all your <u>worries, fears, and discouraging thoughts</u> about your question.

Allow your mind to become radiant by <u>brainstorming encouraging and hopeful ideas</u> about your question. What statements might a best friend, lover, or counselor offer?

CalmUp® Journey

Date: _____

Instructions: Begin in the bottom row. Enter your responses, moving up from left to right.

Deep healing breath; conscious choices **FINISH** → *(1) Today I choose to empower myself by* *(2) I share/serve by*	 _____ Peace & joy rating 1–10 (low to high)
### Spirit	### Spirit
Illusions (First clear your mind on the back of this page.) *I believed*	Creative openings *I open to*
### Society	### Society
Poor choices impacting others *My poor choices have included*	Being of service *With integrity, I will*
### Inward	### Inward
Disheartening image *I have pictured myself*	Self-loving visualization *Today I visualize myself*
### Live	### Live
Disturbing physical symptoms *I have experienced*	Positive affirmation for your health *I am*
### Birth	### Birth
Painful emotions *I have felt*	Peaceful emotions *As my authentic self, I feel*
One issue **START** → *How can I*	 _____ Peace & joy rating 1–10 (low to high)

*Can you conceive that your responses in the left column are not "bad" and those in the right column are not "good"? We need **all** parts of ourselves to create our wholeness.*

Clear your mind by listing or journaling all your <u>worries, fears, and discouraging thoughts</u> about your question.

Allow your mind to become radiant by <u>brainstorming encouraging and hopeful ideas</u> about your question. What statements might a best friend, lover, or counselor offer?

CalmUp® Journey

Date: _____

Instructions: Begin in the bottom row. Enter your responses, moving up from left to right.

<u>Deep healing breath; conscious choices</u> **FINISH** → *(1) Today I choose to empower myself by* *(2) I share/serve by*	 —————— Peace & joy rating 1–10 (low to high)
### Spirit	### Spirit
<u>Illusions</u> (First clear your mind on the back of this page.) *I believed*	<u>Creative openings</u> *I open to*
### Society	### Society
<u>Poor choices impacting others</u> *My poor choices have included*	<u>Being of service</u> *With integrity, I will*
### Inward	### Inward
<u>Disheartening image</u> *I have pictured myself*	<u>Self-loving visualization</u> *Today I visualize myself*
### Live	### Live
<u>Disturbing physical symptoms</u> *I have experienced*	<u>Positive affirmation for your health</u> *I am*
### Birth	### Birth
<u>Painful emotions</u> *I have felt*	<u>Peaceful emotions</u> *As my authentic self, I feel*
<u>One issue</u> **START** → *How can I*	 —————— Peace & joy rating 1–10 (low to high)

Can you conceive that your responses in the left column are not "bad" and those in the right column are not "good"? We need <u>all</u> parts of ourselves to create our wholeness.

Clear your mind by listing or journaling all your <u>worries, fears, and discouraging thoughts</u> about your question.

Allow your mind to become radiant by <u>brainstorming encouraging and hopeful ideas</u> about your question. What statements might a best friend, lover, or counselor offer?

CalmUp® Journey

Date: _____

Instructions: Begin in the bottom row. Enter your responses, moving up from left to right.

Deep healing breath; conscious choices **FINISH** → *(1) Today I choose to empower myself by* *(2) I share/serve by*	 _____ Peace & joy rating 1–10 (low to high)
Spirit	**Spirit**
Illusions (First clear your mind on the back of this page.) *I believed*	Creative openings *I open to*
Society	**Society**
Poor choices impacting others *My poor choices have included*	Being of service *With integrity, I will*
Inward	**Inward**
Disheartening image *I have pictured myself*	Self-loving visualization *Today I visualize myself*
Live	**Live**
Disturbing physical symptoms *I have experienced*	Positive affirmation for your health *I am*
Birth	**Birth**
Painful emotions *I have felt*	Peaceful emotions *As my authentic self, I feel*
One issue **START** → *How can I*	 _____ Peace & joy rating 1–10 (low to high)

Can you conceive that your responses in the left column are not "bad" and those in the right column are not "good"? We need <u>all</u> parts of ourselves to create our wholeness.

Clear your mind by listing or journaling all your <u>worries, fears, and discouraging thoughts</u> about your question.

Allow your mind to become radiant by <u>brainstorming encouraging and hopeful ideas</u> about your question. What statements might a best friend, lover, or counselor offer?

CalmUp® Journey

Date: _____

Instructions: Begin in the bottom row. Enter your responses, moving up from left to right.

Deep healing breath; conscious choices **FINISH** → *(1) Today I choose to empower myself by* *(2) I share/serve by*	 _____ Peace & joy rating 1–10 (low to high)
### Spirit	### Spirit
Illusions (First clear your mind on the back of this page.) *I believed*	Creative openings *I open to*
### Society	### Society
Poor choices impacting others *My poor choices have included*	Being of service *With integrity, I will*
### Inward	### Inward
Disheartening image *I have pictured myself*	Self-loving visualization *Today I visualize myself*
### Live	### Live
Disturbing physical symptoms *I have experienced*	Positive affirmation for your health *I am*
### Birth	### Birth
Painful emotions *I have felt*	Peaceful emotions *As my authentic self, I feel*
One issue **START** → *How can I*	 _____ Peace & joy rating 1–10 (low to high)

*Can you conceive that your responses in the left column are not "bad" and those in the right column are not "good"? We need **all** parts of ourselves to create our wholeness.*

Clear your mind by listing or journaling all your <u>worries, fears, and discouraging thoughts</u> about your question.

Allow your mind to become radiant by <u>brainstorming encouraging and hopeful ideas</u> about your question. What statements might a best friend, lover, or counselor offer?

CalmUp® Journey

Date: _____

Instructions: Begin in the bottom row. Enter your responses, moving up from left to right.

Deep healing breath; conscious choices	
FINISH → *(1) Today I choose to empower myself by* (2) I share/serve by	_____ Peace & joy rating 1–10 (low to high)
Spirit	**Spirit**
Illusions (First clear your mind on the back of this page.) *I believed*	Creative openings *I open to*
Society	**Society**
Poor choices impacting others *My poor choices have included*	Being of service *With integrity, I will*
Inward	**Inward**
Disheartening image *I have pictured myself*	Self-loving visualization *Today I visualize myself*
Live	**Live**
Disturbing physical symptoms *I have experienced*	Positive affirmation for your health *I am*
Birth	**Birth**
Painful emotions *I have felt*	Peaceful emotions *As my authentic self, I feel*
One issue **START** → *How can I*	_____ Peace & joy rating 1–10 (low to high)

*Can you conceive that your responses in the left column are not "bad" and those in the right column are not "good"? We need **all** parts of ourselves to create our wholeness.*

Back Page

Clear your mind by listing or journaling all your <u>worries, fears, and discouraging thoughts</u> about your question.

Allow your mind to become radiant by <u>brainstorming encouraging and hopeful ideas</u> about your question. What statements might a best friend, lover, or counselor offer?

CalmUp® Journey

Date: _____

Instructions: Begin in the bottom row. Enter your responses, moving up from left to right.

<u>Deep healing breath; conscious choices</u> **FINISH** → *(1) Today I choose to empower myself by* *(2) I share/serve by*	 _____ Peace & joy rating 1–10 (low to high)
### Spirit	### Spirit
<u>Illusions</u> (First clear your mind on the back of this page.) *I believed*	<u>Creative openings</u> *I open to*
### Society	### Society
<u>Poor choices impacting others</u> *My poor choices have included*	<u>Being of service</u> *With integrity, I will*
### Inward	### Inward
<u>Disheartening image</u> *I have pictured myself*	<u>Self-loving visualization</u> *Today I visualize myself*
### Live	### Live
<u>Disturbing physical symptoms</u> *I have experienced*	<u>Positive affirmation for your health</u> *I am*
### Birth	### Birth
<u>Painful emotions</u> *I have felt*	<u>Peaceful emotions</u> *As my authentic self, I feel*
<u>One issue</u> **START** → *How can I*	 _____ Peace & joy rating 1–10 (low to high)

Can you conceive that your responses in the left column are not "bad" and those in the right column are not "good"? We need <u>all</u> parts of ourselves to create our wholeness.

Clear your mind by listing or journaling all your <u>worries, fears, and discouraging thoughts</u> about your question.

Allow your mind to become radiant by <u>brainstorming encouraging and hopeful ideas</u> about your question. What statements might a best friend, lover, or counselor offer?

CalmUp® Journey

Date: _____

Instructions: Begin in the bottom row. Enter your responses, moving up from left to right.

<u>Deep healing breath; conscious choices</u> **FINISH** → *(1) Today I choose to empower myself by* *(2) I share/serve by*	 _____ Peace & joy rating 1–10 (low to high)
Spirit	**Spirit**
<u>Illusions</u> (First clear your mind on the back of this page.) *I believed*	<u>Creative openings</u> *I open to*
Society	**Society**
<u>Poor choices impacting others</u> *My poor choices have included*	<u>Being of service</u> *With integrity, I will*
Inward	**Inward**
<u>Disheartening image</u> *I have pictured myself*	<u>Self-loving visualization</u> *Today I visualize myself*
Live	**Live**
<u>Disturbing physical symptoms</u> *I have experienced*	<u>Positive affirmation for your health</u> *I am*
Birth	**Birth**
<u>Painful emotions</u> *I have felt*	<u>Peaceful emotions</u> *As my authentic self, I feel*
<u>One issue</u> **START** → *How can I*	 _____ Peace & joy rating 1–10 (low to high)

Can you conceive that your responses in the left column are not "bad" and those in the right column are not "good"? We need <u>all</u> parts of ourselves to create our wholeness.

Clear your mind by listing or journaling all your <u>worries, fears, and discouraging thoughts</u> about your question.

Allow your mind to become radiant by <u>brainstorming encouraging and hopeful ideas</u> about your question. What statements might a best friend, lover, or counselor offer?

CalmUp® Journey

Date: _____

Instructions: Begin in the bottom row. Enter your responses, moving up from left to right.

<u>Deep healing breath; conscious choices</u> **FINISH** → *(1) Today I choose to empower myself by* *(2) I share/serve by*	 _____ Peace & joy rating 1–10 (low to high)
Spirit	**Spirit**
<u>Illusions</u> (First clear your mind on the back of this page.) *I believed*	<u>Creative openings</u> *I open to*
Society	**Society**
<u>Poor choices impacting others</u> *My poor choices have included*	<u>Being of service</u> *With integrity, I will*
Inward	**Inward**
<u>Disheartening image</u> *I have pictured myself*	<u>Self-loving visualization</u> *Today I visualize myself*
Live	**Live**
<u>Disturbing physical symptoms</u> *I have experienced*	<u>Positive affirmation for your health</u> *I am*
Birth	**Birth**
<u>Painful emotions</u> *I have felt*	<u>Peaceful emotions</u> *As my authentic self, I feel*
<u>One issue</u> **START** → *How can I*	 _____ Peace & joy rating 1–10 (low to high)

Can you conceive that your responses in the left column are not "bad" and those in the right column are not "good"? We need <u>all</u> parts of ourselves to create our wholeness.

Clear your mind by listing or journaling all your <u>worries, fears, and discouraging thoughts</u> about your question.

Allow your mind to become radiant by <u>brainstorming encouraging and hopeful ideas</u> about your question. What statements might a best friend, lover, or counselor offer?

CalmUp® Journey

Date: _____

Instructions: Begin in the bottom row. Enter your responses, moving up from left to right.

Deep healing breath; conscious choices **FINISH** → *(1) Today I choose to empower myself by* *(2) I share/serve by*	 ——— Peace & joy rating 1–10 (low to high)
Spirit	**Spirit**
Illusions (First clear your mind on the back of this page.) *I believed*	Creative openings *I open to*
Society	**Society**
Poor choices impacting others *My poor choices have included*	Being of service *With integrity, I will*
Inward	**Inward**
Disheartening image *I have pictured myself*	Self-loving visualization *Today I visualize myself*
Live	**Live**
Disturbing physical symptoms *I have experienced*	Positive affirmation for your health *I am*
Birth	**Birth**
Painful emotions *I have felt*	Peaceful emotions *As my authentic self, I feel*
One issue **START** → *How can I*	 ——— Peace & joy rating 1–10 (low to high)

Can you conceive that your responses in the left column are not "bad" and those in the right column are not "good"? We need <u>all</u> parts of ourselves to create our wholeness.

Clear your mind by listing or journaling all your worries, fears, and discouraging thoughts about your question.

Allow your mind to become radiant by brainstorming encouraging and hopeful ideas about your question. What statements might a best friend, lover, or counselor offer?

CalmUp® Journey

Date: _____

Instructions: Begin in the bottom row. Enter your responses, moving up from left to right.

<u>Deep healing breath; conscious choices</u> **FINISH** → *(1) Today I choose to empower myself by* *(2) I share/serve by*	 _____ Peace & joy rating 1–10 (low to high)
Spirit	**Spirit**
<u>Illusions</u> (First clear your mind on the back of this page.) *I believed*	<u>Creative openings</u> *I open to*
Society	**Society**
<u>Poor choices impacting others</u> *My poor choices have included*	<u>Being of service</u> *With integrity, I will*
Inward	**Inward**
<u>Disheartening image</u> *I have pictured myself*	<u>Self-loving visualization</u> *Today I visualize myself*
Live	**Live**
<u>Disturbing physical symptoms</u> *I have experienced*	<u>Positive affirmation for your health</u> *I am*
Birth	**Birth**
<u>Painful emotions</u> *I have felt*	<u>Peaceful emotions</u> *As my authentic self, I feel*
<u>One issue</u> **START** → *How can I*	 _____ Peace & joy rating 1–10 (low to high)

Can you conceive that your responses in the left column are not "bad" and those in the right column are not "good"? We need <u>all</u> parts of ourselves to create our wholeness.

Clear your mind by listing or journaling all your <u>worries, fears, and discouraging thoughts</u> about your question.

Allow your mind to become radiant by <u>brainstorming encouraging and hopeful ideas</u> about your question. What statements might a best friend, lover, or counselor offer?

CalmUp® Journey

Date: _____

Instructions: Begin in the bottom row. Enter your responses, moving up from left to right.

<u>Deep healing breath; conscious choices</u> **FINISH** → *(1) Today I choose to empower myself by* *(2) I share/serve by*	 ——————— Peace & joy rating 1–10 (low to high)
Spirit	**Spirit**
<u>Illusions</u> (First clear your mind on the back of this page.) *I believed*	<u>Creative openings</u> *I open to*
Society	**Society**
<u>Poor choices impacting others</u> *My poor choices have included*	<u>Being of service</u> *With integrity, I will*
Inward	**Inward**
<u>Disheartening image</u> *I have pictured myself*	<u>Self-loving visualization</u> *Today I visualize myself*
Live	**Live**
<u>Disturbing physical symptoms</u> *I have experienced*	<u>Positive affirmation for your health</u> *I am*
Birth	**Birth**
<u>Painful emotions</u> *I have felt*	<u>Peaceful emotions</u> *As my authentic self, I feel*
<u>One issue</u> **START** → *How can I*	 ——————— Peace & joy rating 1–10 (low to high)

Can you conceive that your responses in the left column are not "bad" and those in the right column are not "good"? We need <u>all</u> parts of ourselves to create our wholeness.

Clear your mind by listing or journaling all your <u>worries, fears, and discouraging thoughts</u> about your question.

Allow your mind to become radiant by <u>brainstorming encouraging and hopeful ideas</u> about your question. What statements might a best friend, lover, or counselor offer?

CalmUp® Journey

Date: _____

Instructions: Begin in the bottom row. Enter your responses, moving up from left to right.

Deep healing breath; conscious choices **FINISH** → *(1) Today I choose to empower myself by* *(2) I share/serve by*	 _____ Peace & joy rating 1–10 (low to high)
## Spirit	## Spirit
Illusions (First clear your mind on the back of this page.) *I believed*	Creative openings *I open to*
## Society	## Society
Poor choices impacting others *My poor choices have included*	Being of service *With integrity, I will*
## Inward	## Inward
Disheartening image *I have pictured myself*	Self-loving visualization *Today I visualize myself*
## Live	## Live
Disturbing physical symptoms *I have experienced*	Positive affirmation for your health *I am*
## Birth	## Birth
Painful emotions *I have felt*	Peaceful emotions *As my authentic self, I feel*
One issue **START** → *How can I*	 _____ Peace & joy rating 1–10 (low to high)

Can you conceive that your responses in the left column are not "bad" and those in the right column are not "good"? We need __all__ parts of ourselves to create our wholeness.

Clear your mind by listing or journaling all your <u>worries, fears, and discouraging thoughts</u> about your question.

Allow your mind to become radiant by <u>brainstorming encouraging and hopeful ideas</u> about your question. What statements might a best friend, lover, or counselor offer?

CalmUp® Journey

Date: _____

Instructions: Begin in the bottom row. Enter your responses, moving up from left to right.

<u>Deep healing breath; conscious choices</u> **FINISH** → *(1) Today I choose to empower myself by* *(2) I share/serve by*	 ‾‾‾‾‾‾‾ Peace & joy rating 1–10 (low to high)
### Spirit	### Spirit
<u>Illusions</u> (First clear your mind on the back of this page.) *I believed*	<u>Creative openings</u> *I open to*
### Society	### Society
<u>Poor choices impacting others</u> *My poor choices have included*	<u>Being of service</u> *With integrity, I will*
### Inward	### Inward
<u>Disheartening image</u> *I have pictured myself*	<u>Self-loving visualization</u> *Today I visualize myself*
### Live	### Live
<u>Disturbing physical symptoms</u> *I have experienced*	<u>Positive affirmation for your health</u> *I am*
### Birth	### Birth
<u>Painful emotions</u> *I have felt*	<u>Peaceful emotions</u> *As my authentic self, I feel*
<u>One issue</u> **START** → *How can I*	 ‾‾‾‾‾‾‾ Peace & joy rating 1–10 (low to high)

Can you conceive that your responses in the left column are not "bad" and those in the right column are not "good"? We need <u>all</u> parts of ourselves to create our wholeness.

Clear your mind by listing or journaling all your <u>worries, fears, and discouraging thoughts</u> about your question.

Allow your mind to become radiant by <u>brainstorming encouraging and hopeful ideas</u> about your question. What statements might a best friend, lover, or counselor offer?

CalmUp® Journey

Date: _____

Instructions: Begin in the bottom row. Enter your responses, moving up from left to right.

Deep healing breath; conscious choices **FINISH** → *(1) Today I choose to empower myself by* *(2) I share/serve by*	 _____ Peace & joy rating 1–10 (low to high)
Spirit	**Spirit**
Illusions (First clear your mind on the back of this page.) *I believed*	Creative openings *I open to*
Society	**Society**
Poor choices impacting others *My poor choices have included*	Being of service *With integrity, I will*
Inward	**Inward**
Disheartening image *I have pictured myself*	Self-loving visualization *Today I visualize myself*
Live	**Live**
Disturbing physical symptoms *I have experienced*	Positive affirmation for your health *I am*
Birth	**Birth**
Painful emotions *I have felt*	Peaceful emotions *As my authentic self, I feel*
One issue **START** → *How can I*	 _____ Peace & joy rating 1–10 (low to high)

Can you conceive that your responses in the left column are not "bad" and those in the right column are not "good"? We need __all__ parts of ourselves to create our wholeness.

Clear your mind by listing or journaling all your <u>worries, fears, and discouraging thoughts</u> about your question.

Allow your mind to become radiant by <u>brainstorming encouraging and hopeful ideas</u> about your question. What statements might a best friend, lover, or counselor offer?

CalmUp® Journey

Date: _____

Instructions: Begin in the bottom row. Enter your responses, moving up from left to right.

Deep healing breath; conscious choices **FINISH** → *(1) Today I choose to empower myself by* *(2) I share/serve by*	_____ Peace & joy rating 1–10 (low to high)
Spirit	**Spirit**
Illusions (First clear your mind on the back of this page.) *I believed*	Creative openings *I open to*
Society	**Society**
Poor choices impacting others *My poor choices have included*	Being of service *With integrity, I will*
Inward	**Inward**
Disheartening image *I have pictured myself*	Self-loving visualization *Today I visualize myself*
Live	**Live**
Disturbing physical symptoms *I have experienced*	Positive affirmation for your health *I am*
Birth	**Birth**
Painful emotions *I have felt*	Peaceful emotions *As my authentic self, I feel*
One issue **START** → *How can I*	_____ Peace & joy rating 1–10 (low to high)

Can you conceive that your responses in the left column are not "bad" and those in the right column are not "good"? We need <u>all</u> parts of ourselves to create our wholeness.

Clear your mind by listing or journaling all your <u>worries, fears, and discouraging thoughts</u> about your question.

Allow your mind to become radiant by <u>brainstorming encouraging and hopeful ideas</u> about your question. What statements might a best friend, lover, or counselor offer?

CalmUp® Journey

Date: _____

Instructions: Begin in the bottom row. Enter your responses, moving up from left to right.

Deep healing breath; conscious choices **FINISH** → *(1) Today I choose to empower myself by* *(2) I share/serve by*	 _____ Peace & joy rating 1–10 (low to high)
Spirit	**Spirit**
Illusions (First clear your mind on the back of this page.) *I believed*	Creative openings *I open to*
Society	**Society**
Poor choices impacting others *My poor choices have included*	Being of service *With integrity, I will*
Inward	**Inward**
Disheartening image *I have pictured myself*	Self-loving visualization *Today I visualize myself*
Live	**Live**
Disturbing physical symptoms *I have experienced*	Positive affirmation for your health *I am*
Birth	**Birth**
Painful emotions *I have felt*	Peaceful emotions *As my authentic self, I feel*
One issue **START** → *How can I*	 _____ Peace & joy rating 1–10 (low to high)

Can you conceive that your responses in the left column are not "bad" and those in the right column are not "good"? We need all parts of ourselves to create our wholeness.

Clear your mind by listing or journaling all your <u>worries, fears, and discouraging thoughts</u> about your question.

Allow your mind to become radiant by <u>brainstorming encouraging and hopeful ideas</u> about your question. What statements might a best friend, lover, or counselor offer?

CalmUp® Journey

Date: _____

Instructions: Begin in the bottom row. Enter your responses, moving up from left to right.

<u>Deep healing breath; conscious choices</u> **FINISH** → *(1) Today I choose to empower myself by* *(2) I share/serve by*	 _____ Peace & joy rating 1–10 (low to high)
### Spirit	### Spirit
<u>Illusions</u> (First clear your mind on the back of this page.) *I believed*	<u>Creative openings</u> *I open to*
### Society	### Society
<u>Poor choices impacting others</u> *My poor choices have included*	<u>Being of service</u> *With integrity, I will*
### Inward	### Inward
<u>Disheartening image</u> *I have pictured myself*	<u>Self-loving visualization</u> *Today I visualize myself*
### Live	### Live
<u>Disturbing physical symptoms</u> *I have experienced*	<u>Positive affirmation for your health</u> *I am*
### Birth	### Birth
<u>Painful emotions</u> *I have felt*	<u>Peaceful emotions</u> *As my authentic self, I feel*
<u>One issue</u> **START** → *How can I*	 _____ Peace & joy rating 1–10 (low to high)

Can you conceive that your responses in the left column are not "bad" and those in the right column are not "good"? We need <u>all</u> parts of ourselves to create our wholeness.

Clear your mind by listing or journaling all your <u>worries, fears, and discouraging thoughts</u> about your question.

Allow your mind to become radiant by <u>brainstorming encouraging and hopeful ideas</u> about your question. What statements might a best friend, lover, or counselor offer?

CalmUp® Journey

Date: _____

Instructions: Begin in the bottom row. Enter your responses, moving up from left to right.

Deep healing breath; conscious choices **FINISH** → *(1) Today I choose to empower myself by* *(2) I share/serve by*	 _____ Peace & joy rating 1–10 (low to high)
## Spirit	## Spirit
Illusions (First clear your mind on the back of this page.) *I believed*	Creative openings *I open to*
## Society	## Society
Poor choices impacting others *My poor choices have included*	Being of service *With integrity, I will*
## Inward	## Inward
Disheartening image *I have pictured myself*	Self-loving visualization *Today I visualize myself*
## Live	## Live
Disturbing physical symptoms *I have experienced*	Positive affirmation for your health *I am*
## Birth	## Birth
Painful emotions *I have felt*	Peaceful emotions *As my authentic self, I feel*
One issue **START** → *How can I*	 _____ Peace & joy rating 1–10 (low to high)

Can you conceive that your responses in the left column are not "bad" and those in the right column are not "good"? We need __all__ parts of ourselves to create our wholeness.

Clear your mind by listing or journaling all your <u>worries, fears, and discouraging thoughts</u> about your question.

Allow your mind to become radiant by <u>brainstorming encouraging and hopeful ideas</u> about your question. What statements might a best friend, lover, or counselor offer?

CalmUp® Journey

Date: _____

Instructions: Begin in the bottom row. Enter your responses, moving up from left to right.

<u>Deep healing breath; conscious choices</u> **FINISH** → *(1) Today I choose to empower myself by* *(2) I share/serve by*	 _____ Peace & joy rating 1–10 (low to high)
Spirit	**Spirit**
<u>Illusions</u> (First clear your mind on the back of this page.) *I believed*	<u>Creative openings</u> *I open to*
Society	**Society**
<u>Poor choices impacting others</u> *My poor choices have included*	<u>Being of service</u> *With integrity, I will*
Inward	**Inward**
<u>Disheartening image</u> *I have pictured myself*	<u>Self-loving visualization</u> *Today I visualize myself*
Live	**Live**
<u>Disturbing physical symptoms</u> *I have experienced*	<u>Positive affirmation for your health</u> *I am*
Birth	**Birth**
<u>Painful emotions</u> *I have felt*	<u>Peaceful emotions</u> *As my authentic self, I feel*
<u>One issue</u> **START** → *How can I*	 _____ Peace & joy rating 1–10 (low to high)

Can you conceive that your responses in the left column are not "bad" and those in the right column are not "good"? We need <u>all</u> parts of ourselves to create our wholeness.

Clear your mind by listing or journaling all your <u>worries, fears, and discouraging thoughts</u> about your question.

Allow your mind to become radiant by <u>brainstorming encouraging and hopeful ideas</u> about your question. What statements might a best friend, lover, or counselor offer?

CalmUp® Journey

Date: _____

Instructions: Begin in the bottom row. Enter your responses, moving up from left to right.

<u>Deep healing breath; conscious choices</u> **FINISH →** *(1) Today I choose to empower myself by* *(2) I share/serve by*	 _____ Peace & joy rating 1–10 (low to high)
Spirit	**Spirit**
<u>Illusions</u> (First clear your mind on the back of this page.) *I believed*	<u>Creative openings</u> *I open to*
Society	**Society**
<u>Poor choices impacting others</u> *My poor choices have included*	<u>Being of service</u> *With integrity, I will*
Inward	**Inward**
<u>Disheartening image</u> *I have pictured myself*	<u>Self-loving visualization</u> *Today I visualize myself*
Live	**Live**
<u>Disturbing physical symptoms</u> *I have experienced*	<u>Positive affirmation for your health</u> *I am*
Birth	**Birth**
<u>Painful emotions</u> *I have felt*	<u>Peaceful emotions</u> *As my authentic self, I feel*
<u>One issue</u> **START →** *How can I*	 _____ Peace & joy rating 1–10 (low to high)

Can you conceive that your responses in the left column are not "bad" and those in the right column are not "good"? We need <u>all</u> parts of ourselves to create our wholeness.

Clear your mind by listing or journaling all your <u>worries, fears, and discouraging thoughts</u> about your question.

Allow your mind to become radiant by <u>brainstorming encouraging and hopeful ideas</u> about your question. What statements might a best friend, lover, or counselor offer?

CalmUp® Journey

Date: _____

Instructions: Begin in the bottom row. Enter your responses, moving up from left to right.

Deep healing breath; conscious choices **FINISH →** *(1) Today I choose to empower myself by* *(2) I share/serve by*	 _____ Peace & joy rating 1–10 (low to high)
Spirit	**Spirit**
Illusions (First clear your mind on the back of this page.) *I believed*	Creative openings *I open to*
Society	**Society**
Poor choices impacting others *My poor choices have included*	Being of service *With integrity, I will*
Inward	**Inward**
Disheartening image *I have pictured myself*	Self-loving visualization *Today I visualize myself*
Live	**Live**
Disturbing physical symptoms *I have experienced*	Positive affirmation for your health *I am*
Birth	**Birth**
Painful emotions *I have felt*	Peaceful emotions *As my authentic self, I feel*
One issue **START →** *How can I*	 _____ Peace & joy rating 1–10 (low to high)

Can you conceive that your responses in the left column are not "bad" and those in the right column are not "good"? We need __all__ parts of ourselves to create our wholeness.

Clear your mind by listing or journaling all your <u>worries, fears, and discouraging thoughts</u> about your question.

Allow your mind to become radiant by <u>brainstorming encouraging and hopeful ideas</u> about your question. What statements might a best friend, lover, or counselor offer?

CalmUp® Journey

Date: _____

Instructions: Begin in the bottom row. Enter your responses, moving up from left to right.

Deep healing breath; conscious choices **FINISH →** *(1) Today I choose to empower myself by* *(2) I share/serve by*	 ‾‾‾‾‾‾ Peace & joy rating 1–10 (low to high)
Spirit	**Spirit**
Illusions (First clear your mind on the back of this page.) *I believed*	Creative openings *I open to*
Society	**Society**
Poor choices impacting others *My poor choices have included*	Being of service *With integrity, I will*
Inward	**Inward**
Disheartening image *I have pictured myself*	Self-loving visualization *Today I visualize myself*
Live	**Live**
Disturbing physical symptoms *I have experienced*	Positive affirmation for your health *I am*
Birth	**Birth**
Painful emotions *I have felt*	Peaceful emotions *As my authentic self, I feel*
One issue **START →** *How can I*	 ‾‾‾‾‾‾ Peace & joy rating 1–10 (low to high)

Can you conceive that your responses in the left column are not "bad" and those in the right column are not "good"? We need __all__ parts of ourselves to create our wholeness.

Back Page

Clear your mind by listing or journaling all your <u>worries, fears, and discouraging thoughts</u> about your question.

Allow your mind to become radiant by <u>brainstorming encouraging and hopeful ideas</u> about your question. What statements might a best friend, lover, or counselor offer?

CalmUp® Journey

Date: _____

Instructions: Begin in the bottom row. Enter your responses, moving up from left to right.

<u>Deep healing breath; conscious choices</u> **FINISH** → *(1) Today I choose to empower myself by* *(2) I share/serve by*	 ———————— Peace & joy rating 1–10 (low to high)
Spirit	**Spirit**
<u>Illusions</u> (First clear your mind on the back of this page.) *I believed*	<u>Creative openings</u> *I open to*
Society	**Society**
<u>Poor choices impacting others</u> *My poor choices have included*	<u>Being of service</u> *With integrity, I will*
Inward	**Inward**
<u>Disheartening image</u> *I have pictured myself*	<u>Self-loving visualization</u> *Today I visualize myself*
Live	**Live**
<u>Disturbing physical symptoms</u> *I have experienced*	<u>Positive affirmation for your health</u> *I am*
Birth	**Birth**
<u>Painful emotions</u> *I have felt*	<u>Peaceful emotions</u> *As my authentic self, I feel*
<u>One issue</u> **START** → *How can I*	 ———————— Peace & joy rating 1–10 (low to high)

Can you conceive that your responses in the left column are not "bad" and those in the right column are not "good"? We need <u>all</u> parts of ourselves to create our wholeness.

Clear your mind by listing or journaling all your <u>worries, fears, and discouraging thoughts</u> about your question.

Allow your mind to become radiant by <u>brainstorming encouraging and hopeful ideas</u> about your question. What statements might a best friend, lover, or counselor offer?

CalmUp® Journey

Date: _____

Instructions: Begin in the bottom row. Enter your responses, moving up from left to right.

<u>Deep healing breath; conscious choices</u> **FINISH** → *(1) Today I choose to empower myself by* *(2) I share/serve by*	 ———— Peace & joy rating 1–10 (low to high)
## Spirit	## Spirit
<u>Illusions</u> (First clear your mind on the back of this page.) *I believed*	<u>Creative openings</u> *I open to*
## Society	## Society
<u>Poor choices impacting others</u> *My poor choices have included*	<u>Being of service</u> *With integrity, I will*
## Inward	## Inward
<u>Disheartening image</u> *I have pictured myself*	<u>Self-loving visualization</u> *Today I visualize myself*
## Live	## Live
<u>Disturbing physical symptoms</u> *I have experienced*	<u>Positive affirmation for your health</u> *I am*
## Birth	## Birth
<u>Painful emotions</u> *I have felt*	<u>Peaceful emotions</u> *As my authentic self, I feel*
<u>One issue</u> **START** → *How can I*	 ———— Peace & joy rating 1–10 (low to high)

*Can you conceive that your responses in the left column are not "bad" and those in the right column are not "good"? We need **all** parts of ourselves to create our wholeness.*

Clear your mind by listing or journaling all your <u>worries, fears, and discouraging thoughts</u> about your question.

Allow your mind to become radiant by <u>brainstorming encouraging and hopeful ideas</u> about your question. What statements might a best friend, lover, or counselor offer?

CalmUp® Journey

Date: _____

Instructions: Begin in the bottom row. Enter your responses, moving up from left to right.

<u>Deep healing breath; conscious choices</u> **FINISH** → *(1) Today I choose to empower myself by* *(2) I share/serve by*	 _____ Peace & joy rating 1–10 (low to high)
Spirit	**Spirit**
<u>Illusions</u> (First clear your mind on the back of this page.) *I believed*	<u>Creative openings</u> *I open to*
Society	**Society**
<u>Poor choices impacting others</u> *My poor choices have included*	<u>Being of service</u> *With integrity, I will*
Inward	**Inward**
<u>Disheartening image</u> *I have pictured myself*	<u>Self-loving visualization</u> *Today I visualize myself*
Live	**Live**
<u>Disturbing physical symptoms</u> *I have experienced*	<u>Positive affirmation for your health</u> *I am*
Birth	**Birth**
<u>Painful emotions</u> *I have felt*	<u>Peaceful emotions</u> *As my authentic self, I feel*
<u>One issue</u> **START** → *How can I*	 _____ Peace & joy rating 1–10 (low to high)

Can you conceive that your responses in the left column are not "bad" and those in the right column are not "good"? We need <u>all</u> parts of ourselves to create our wholeness.

Clear your mind by listing or journaling all your <u>worries, fears, and discouraging thoughts</u> about your question.

Allow your mind to become radiant by <u>brainstorming encouraging and hopeful ideas</u> about your question. What statements might a best friend, lover, or counselor offer?

CalmUp® Journey

Date: _____

Instructions: Begin in the bottom row. Enter your responses, moving up from left to right.

<u>Deep healing breath; conscious choices</u> **FINISH →** *(1) Today I choose to empower myself by* *(2) I share/serve by*	 _____ Peace & joy rating 1–10 (low to high)
### Spirit	### Spirit
<u>Illusions</u> (First clear your mind on the back of this page.) *I believed*	<u>Creative openings</u> *I open to*
### Society	### Society
<u>Poor choices impacting others</u> *My poor choices have included*	<u>Being of service</u> *With integrity, I will*
### Inward	### Inward
<u>Disheartening image</u> *I have pictured myself*	<u>Self-loving visualization</u> *Today I visualize myself*
### Live	### Live
<u>Disturbing physical symptoms</u> *I have experienced*	<u>Positive affirmation for your health</u> *I am*
### Birth	### Birth
<u>Painful emotions</u> *I have felt*	<u>Peaceful emotions</u> *As my authentic self, I feel*
<u>One issue</u> **START →** *How can I*	 _____ Peace & joy rating 1–10 (low to high)

Can you conceive that your responses in the left column are not "bad" and those in the right column are not "good"? We need <u>all</u> parts of ourselves to create our wholeness.

Clear your mind by listing or journaling all your <u>worries, fears, and discouraging thoughts</u> about your question.

Allow your mind to become radiant by <u>brainstorming encouraging and hopeful ideas</u> about your question. What statements might a best friend, lover, or counselor offer?

CalmUp® Journey

Date: _____

Instructions: Begin in the bottom row. Enter your responses, moving up from left to right.

<u>Deep healing breath; conscious choices</u> **FINISH** → *(1) Today I choose to empower myself by* *(2) I share/serve by*	 _____ Peace & joy rating 1–10 (low to high)
### Spirit	### Spirit
<u>Illusions</u> (First clear your mind on the back of this page.) *I believed*	<u>Creative openings</u> *I open to*
### Society	### Society
<u>Poor choices impacting others</u> *My poor choices have included*	<u>Being of service</u> *With integrity, I will*
### Inward	### Inward
<u>Disheartening image</u> *I have pictured myself*	<u>Self-loving visualization</u> *Today I visualize myself*
### Live	### Live
<u>Disturbing physical symptoms</u> *I have experienced*	<u>Positive affirmation for your health</u> *I am*
### Birth	### Birth
<u>Painful emotions</u> *I have felt*	<u>Peaceful emotions</u> *As my authentic self, I feel*
<u>One issue</u> **START** → *How can I*	 _____ Peace & joy rating 1–10 (low to high)

Can you conceive that your responses in the left column are not "bad" and those in the right column are not "good"? We need <u>all</u> parts of ourselves to create our wholeness.

Clear your mind by listing or journaling all your <u>worries, fears, and discouraging thoughts</u> about your question.

Allow your mind to become radiant by <u>brainstorming encouraging and hopeful ideas</u> about your question. What statements might a best friend, lover, or counselor offer?

CalmUp® Journey

Date: _____

Instructions: Begin in the bottom row. Enter your responses, moving up from left to right.

Deep healing breath; conscious choices **FINISH** → *(1) Today I choose to empower myself by* *(2) I share/serve by*	 _____ Peace & joy rating 1–10 (low to high)
Spirit	**Spirit**
Illusions (First clear your mind on the back of this page.) *I believed*	Creative openings *I open to*
Society	**Society**
Poor choices impacting others *My poor choices have included*	Being of service *With integrity, I will*
Inward	**Inward**
Disheartening image *I have pictured myself*	Self-loving visualization *Today I visualize myself*
Live	**Live**
Disturbing physical symptoms *I have experienced*	Positive affirmation for your health *I am*
Birth	**Birth**
Painful emotions *I have felt*	Peaceful emotions *As my authentic self, I feel*
One issue **START** → *How can I*	 _____ Peace & joy rating 1–10 (low to high)

Can you conceive that your responses in the left column are not "bad" and those in the right column are not "good"? We need <u>all</u> parts of ourselves to create our wholeness.

Clear your mind by listing or journaling all your <u>worries, fears, and discouraging thoughts</u> about your question.

Allow your mind to become radiant by <u>brainstorming encouraging and hopeful ideas</u> about your question. What statements might a best friend, lover, or counselor offer?

CalmUp® Journey

Date: _____

Instructions: Begin in the bottom row. Enter your responses, moving up from left to right.

Deep healing breath; conscious choices **FINISH** → *(1) Today I choose to empower myself by* *(2) I share/serve by*	 _____ Peace & joy rating 1–10 (low to high)
Spirit	**Spirit**
Illusions (First clear your mind on the back of this page.) *I believed*	Creative openings *I open to*
Society	**Society**
Poor choices impacting others *My poor choices have included*	Being of service *With integrity, I will*
Inward	**Inward**
Disheartening image *I have pictured myself*	Self-loving visualization *Today I visualize myself*
Live	**Live**
Disturbing physical symptoms *I have experienced*	Positive affirmation for your health *I am*
Birth	**Birth**
Painful emotions *I have felt*	Peaceful emotions *As my authentic self, I feel*
One issue **START** → *How can I*	 _____ Peace & joy rating 1–10 (low to high)

Can you conceive that your responses in the left column are not "bad" and those in the right column are not "good"? We need all parts of ourselves to create our wholeness.

Clear your mind by listing or journaling all your <u>worries, fears, and discouraging thoughts</u> about your question.

Allow your mind to become radiant by <u>brainstorming encouraging and hopeful ideas</u> about your question. What statements might a best friend, lover, or counselor offer?

CalmUp® Journey

Date: _____

Instructions: Begin in the bottom row. Enter your responses, moving up from left to right.

Deep healing breath; conscious choices **FINISH** → *(1) Today I choose to empower myself by* *(2) I share/serve by*	 _____ Peace & joy rating 1–10 (low to high)
Spirit	**Spirit**
Illusions (First clear your mind on the back of this page.) *I believed*	Creative openings *I open to*
Society	**Society**
Poor choices impacting others *My poor choices have included*	Being of service *With integrity, I will*
Inward	**Inward**
Disheartening image *I have pictured myself*	Self-loving visualization *Today I visualize myself*
Live	**Live**
Disturbing physical symptoms *I have experienced*	Positive affirmation for your health *I am*
Birth	**Birth**
Painful emotions *I have felt*	Peaceful emotions *As my authentic self, I feel*
One issue **START** → *How can I*	 _____ Peace & joy rating 1–10 (low to high)

Can you conceive that your responses in the left column are not "bad" and those in the right column are not "good"? We need __all__ parts of ourselves to create our wholeness.

Clear your mind by listing or journaling all your <u>worries, fears, and discouraging thoughts</u> about your question.

Allow your mind to become radiant by <u>brainstorming encouraging and hopeful ideas</u> about your question. What statements might a best friend, lover, or counselor offer?

CalmUp® Journey

Date: _____

Instructions: Begin in the bottom row. Enter your responses, moving up from left to right.

<u>Deep healing breath; conscious choices</u> **FINISH** → *(1) Today I choose to empower myself by* *(2) I share/serve by*	 _____ Peace & joy rating 1–10 (low to high)
Spirit	**Spirit**
<u>Illusions</u> (First clear your mind on the back of this page.) *I believed*	<u>Creative openings</u> *I open to*
Society	**Society**
<u>Poor choices impacting others</u> *My poor choices have included*	<u>Being of service</u> *With integrity, I will*
Inward	**Inward**
<u>Disheartening image</u> *I have pictured myself*	<u>Self-loving visualization</u> *Today I visualize myself*
Live	**Live**
<u>Disturbing physical symptoms</u> *I have experienced*	<u>Positive affirmation for your health</u> *I am*
Birth	**Birth**
<u>Painful emotions</u> *I have felt*	<u>Peaceful emotions</u> *As my authentic self, I feel*
<u>One issue</u> **START** → *How can I*	 _____ Peace & joy rating 1–10 (low to high)

Can you conceive that your responses in the left column are not "bad" and those in the right column are not "good"? We need <u>all</u> parts of ourselves to create our wholeness.

Clear your mind by listing or journaling all your <u>worries, fears, and discouraging thoughts</u> about your question.

Allow your mind to become radiant by <u>brainstorming encouraging and hopeful ideas</u> about your question. What statements might a best friend, lover, or counselor offer?

CalmUp® Journey

Date: _____

Instructions: Begin in the bottom row. Enter your responses, moving up from left to right.

<u>Deep healing breath; conscious choices</u> **FINISH** → *(1) Today I choose to empower myself by* *(2) I share/serve by*	 ———— Peace & joy rating 1–10 (low to high)
Spirit	**Spirit**
<u>Illusions</u> (First clear your mind on the back of this page.) *I believed*	<u>Creative openings</u> *I open to*
Society	**Society**
<u>Poor choices impacting others</u> *My poor choices have included*	<u>Being of service</u> *With integrity, I will*
Inward	**Inward**
<u>Disheartening image</u> *I have pictured myself*	<u>Self-loving visualization</u> *Today I visualize myself*
Live	**Live**
<u>Disturbing physical symptoms</u> *I have experienced*	<u>Positive affirmation for your health</u> *I am*
Birth	**Birth**
<u>Painful emotions</u> *I have felt*	<u>Peaceful emotions</u> *As my authentic self, I feel*
<u>One issue</u> **START** → *How can I*	 ———— Peace & joy rating 1–10 (low to high)

Can you conceive that your responses in the left column are not "bad" and those in the right column are not "good"? We need <u>all</u> parts of ourselves to create our wholeness.

Clear your mind by listing or journaling all your <u>worries, fears, and discouraging thoughts</u> about your question.

Allow your mind to become radiant by <u>brainstorming encouraging and hopeful ideas</u> about your question. What statements might a best friend, lover, or counselor offer?

CalmUp® Journey

Date: _____

Instructions: Begin in the bottom row. Enter your responses, moving up from left to right.

Deep healing breath; conscious choices **FINISH** → *(1) Today I choose to empower myself by* *(2) I share/serve by*	 _____ Peace & joy rating 1–10 (low to high)
Spirit	**Spirit**
Illusions (First clear your mind on the back of this page.) *I believed*	Creative openings *I open to*
Society	**Society**
Poor choices impacting others *My poor choices have included*	Being of service *With integrity, I will*
Inward	**Inward**
Disheartening image *I have pictured myself*	Self-loving visualization *Today I visualize myself*
Live	**Live**
Disturbing physical symptoms *I have experienced*	Positive affirmation for your health *I am*
Birth	**Birth**
Painful emotions *I have felt*	Peaceful emotions *As my authentic self, I feel*
One issue **START** → *How can I*	 _____ Peace & joy rating 1–10 (low to high)

Can you conceive that your responses in the left column are not "bad" and those in the right column are not "good"? We need __all__ parts of ourselves to create our wholeness.

Clear your mind by listing or journaling all your <u>worries, fears, and discouraging thoughts</u> about your question.

Allow your mind to become radiant by <u>brainstorming encouraging and hopeful ideas</u> about your question. What statements might a best friend, lover, or counselor offer?

CalmUp® Journey

Date: _____

Instructions: Begin in the bottom row. Enter your responses, moving up from left to right.

Deep healing breath; conscious choices **FINISH** → *(1) Today I choose to empower myself by* *(2) I share/serve by*	 _____ Peace & joy rating 1–10 (low to high)
Spirit	**Spirit**
Illusions (First clear your mind on the back of this page.) *I believed*	Creative openings *I open to*
Society	**Society**
Poor choices impacting others *My poor choices have included*	Being of service *With integrity, I will*
Inward	**Inward**
Disheartening image *I have pictured myself*	Self-loving visualization *Today I visualize myself*
Live	**Live**
Disturbing physical symptoms *I have experienced*	Positive affirmation for your health *I am*
Birth	**Birth**
Painful emotions *I have felt*	Peaceful emotions *As my authentic self, I feel*
One issue **START** → *How can I*	 _____ Peace & joy rating 1–10 (low to high)

*Can you conceive that your responses in the left column are not "bad" and those in the right column are not "good"? We need **all** parts of ourselves to create our wholeness.*

Clear your mind by listing or journaling all your <u>worries, fears, and discouraging thoughts</u> about your question.

Allow your mind to become radiant by <u>brainstorming encouraging and hopeful ideas</u> about your question. What statements might a best friend, lover, or counselor offer?

CalmUp® Journey

Date: _____

Instructions: Begin in the bottom row. Enter your responses, moving up from left to right.

<u>Deep healing breath; conscious choices</u> **FINISH** → *(1) Today I choose to empower myself by* *(2) I share/serve by*	 _____ Peace & joy rating 1–10 (low to high)
## Spirit	## Spirit
<u>Illusions</u> (First clear your mind on the back of this page.) *I believed*	<u>Creative openings</u> *I open to*
## Society	## Society
<u>Poor choices impacting others</u> *My poor choices have included*	<u>Being of service</u> *With integrity, I will*
## Inward	## Inward
<u>Disheartening image</u> *I have pictured myself*	<u>Self-loving visualization</u> *Today I visualize myself*
## Live	## Live
<u>Disturbing physical symptoms</u> *I have experienced*	<u>Positive affirmation for your health</u> *I am*
## Birth	## Birth
<u>Painful emotions</u> *I have felt*	<u>Peaceful emotions</u> *As my authentic self, I feel*
<u>One issue</u> **START** → *How can I*	 _____ Peace & joy rating 1–10 (low to high)

Can you conceive that your responses in the left column are not "bad" and those in the right column are not "good"? We need <u>all</u> parts of ourselves to create our wholeness.

Clear your mind by listing or journaling all your <u>worries, fears, and discouraging thoughts</u> about your question.

Allow your mind to become radiant by <u>brainstorming encouraging and hopeful ideas</u> about your question. What statements might a best friend, lover, or counselor offer?

CalmUp® Journey

Date: _____

Instructions: Begin in the bottom row. Enter your responses, moving up from left to right.

Deep healing breath; conscious choices **FINISH** → *(1) Today I choose to empower myself by* *(2) I share/serve by*	 _____ Peace & joy rating 1–10 (low to high)
Spirit	**Spirit**
Illusions (First clear your mind on the back of this page.) *I believed*	Creative openings *I open to*
Society	**Society**
Poor choices impacting others *My poor choices have included*	Being of service *With integrity, I will*
Inward	**Inward**
Disheartening image *I have pictured myself*	Self-loving visualization *Today I visualize myself*
Live	**Live**
Disturbing physical symptoms *I have experienced*	Positive affirmation for your health *I am*
Birth	**Birth**
Painful emotions *I have felt*	Peaceful emotions *As my authentic self, I feel*
One issue **START** → *How can I*	 _____ Peace & joy rating 1–10 (low to high)

Can you conceive that your responses in the left column are not "bad" and those in the right column are not "good"? We need all parts of ourselves to create our wholeness.

Clear your mind by listing or journaling all your <u>worries, fears, and discouraging thoughts</u> about your question.

Allow your mind to become radiant by <u>brainstorming encouraging and hopeful ideas</u> about your question. What statements might a best friend, lover, or counselor offer?

CalmUp® Journey

Date: _____

Instructions: Begin in the bottom row. Enter your responses, moving up from left to right.

<u>Deep healing breath; conscious choices</u> **FINISH** → *(1) Today I choose to empower myself by* *(2) I share/serve by*	 ——————— <u>Peace & joy rating 1–10 (low to high)</u>
Spirit	**Spirit**
<u>Illusions</u> (First clear your mind on the back of this page.) *I believed*	<u>Creative openings</u> *I open to*
Society	**Society**
<u>Poor choices impacting others</u> *My poor choices have included*	<u>Being of service</u> *With integrity, I will*
Inward	**Inward**
<u>Disheartening image</u> *I have pictured myself*	<u>Self-loving visualization</u> *Today I visualize myself*
Live	**Live**
<u>Disturbing physical symptoms</u> *I have experienced*	<u>Positive affirmation for your health</u> *I am*
Birth	**Birth**
<u>Painful emotions</u> *I have felt*	<u>Peaceful emotions</u> *As my authentic self, I feel*
<u>One issue</u> **START** → *How can I*	 ——————— <u>Peace & joy rating 1–10 (low to high)</u>

Can you conceive that your responses in the left column are not "bad" and those in the right column are not "good"? We need <u>all</u> parts of ourselves to create our wholeness.

Clear your mind by listing or journaling all your <u>worries, fears, and discouraging thoughts</u> about your question.

Allow your mind to become radiant by <u>brainstorming encouraging and hopeful ideas</u> about your question. What statements might a best friend, lover, or counselor offer?

CalmUp® Journey

Date: _____

Instructions: Begin in the bottom row. Enter your responses, moving up from left to right.

<u>Deep healing breath; conscious choices</u> **FINISH** → *(1) Today I choose to empower myself by* *(2) I share/serve by*	 _____ Peace & joy rating 1–10 (low to high)
Spirit	**Spirit**
<u>Illusions</u> (First clear your mind on the back of this page.) *I believed*	<u>Creative openings</u> *I open to*
Society	**Society**
<u>Poor choices impacting others</u> *My poor choices have included*	<u>Being of service</u> *With integrity, I will*
Inward	**Inward**
<u>Disheartening image</u> *I have pictured myself*	<u>Self-loving visualization</u> *Today I visualize myself*
Live	**Live**
<u>Disturbing physical symptoms</u> *I have experienced*	<u>Positive affirmation for your health</u> *I am*
Birth	**Birth**
<u>Painful emotions</u> *I have felt*	<u>Peaceful emotions</u> *As my authentic self, I feel*
<u>One issue</u> **START** → *How can I*	 _____ Peace & joy rating 1–10 (low to high)

Can you conceive that your responses in the left column are not "bad" and those in the right column are not "good"? We need <u>all</u> parts of ourselves to create our wholeness.

Clear your mind by listing or journaling all your <u>worries, fears, and discouraging thoughts</u> about your question.

Allow your mind to become radiant by <u>brainstorming encouraging and hopeful ideas</u> about your question. What statements might a best friend, lover, or counselor offer?